The Hospitality of Ministry

The Hospitality of Ministry

Exercising Christian Ministry with a Trinitarian Heart

David Ranson

ST PAULS

THE HOSPITALITY OF MINISTRY:
Exercising Christian Ministry with a Trinitarian Heart

© David Ranson, 2012

Acknowledgments:
Scripture quotations are from THE HOLY BIBLE, NEW INTERNATIONAL VERSION®, NIV® Copyright © 1973, 1978, 1984, 2011 by Biblica, Inc.™ Used by permission. All rights reserved worldwide.

Cover painting: The Hospitality of Abraham, by Andrei Rublev (ca. 1410). Digital image © (2012) The Museum of Modern Art/Scala, Florence. Reproduced with permission.

National Library of Australia Cataloguing-in-Publication entry

Author: Ranson, David, 1959-
Title: The hospitality of ministry : exercising Christian
             ministry with a trinitarian heart / David Ranson.
ISBN: 9781921963063 (pbk.)
Subjects: Pastoral theology.
             Trinity.
Dewey Number: 253

Published in 2012 by
ST PAULS PUBLICATIONS—Society of St Paul
PO Box 906, Strathfield NSW 2135, Australia
http://www.stpauls.com.au

Cover design by Domenika Fairy

Printed in China by Everbest

ST PAULS PUBLICATIONS is an activity of the priests and brothers of the Society of St Paul who place at the centre of their lives the mission of evangelisation through the modern means of social communication.

Dedicated to
Alex Nelson
whose guidance is beyond value
and to
my brother priests
and the many ecclesial ministers
of the Diocese of Broken Bay

You, therefore, God the Father,
by whom as Creator we live;
You, Wisdom of the Father,
by whom we have been made anew and taught to live wisely;
You, Holy Spirit, whom and in whom we love and so live
happily,
and are to live yet more so;
You, who are Three in one Substance,
the one God,
from whom we are
by whom we are
in whom we are;
You, from whom we departed by sinning,
to whom we were made unlike,
but away from whom we have not been allowed to perish;
You the Beginning to whom we are returning,
the Pattern we are following,
the Grace by which we are reconciled:
You we worship and bless!
To you be glory forever!

Amen

William of St. Thierry, *De Contemplando Dei, On Contemplating God*, translated by P. Lawson. Cistercian Fathers Series 3 (Spencer, MA: Cistercian Publications, 1971), 63.

CONTENTS

INTRODUCTION

The centrality of the Trinity to our life of faith, and its fundamental importance to our life of ministry, cannot be underestimated. Indeed, it is a mark of our own time that there is a certain 'renewal or renaissance of Trinitarian theology.'[1] Given that it is often through art that the Divine Mystery manifests its truth most evocatively for us, it is not, surprising, therefore that there has been a retrieval of the classic icons of the Trinity. The icon, I believe, that depicts this Triune Mystery most powerfully is the one painted by Andrei Rublev in 1425, 'The Hospitality of Abraham.'[2] It was formed not only to share the fruits of his own meditation but also in order to offer his fellow monks a way to keep their hearts centered in God during a time of significant change. As we gaze upon the icon in our own time, we place ourselves before the same Mystery in such a way that it might shed fresh light on our ministry in our own challenging context. We can allow our gaze to be drawn through the window which the icon provides, and allow the Triune Mystery to draw us into itself so that it might ever so gently disclose its truth and beauty to us anew. It may then captivate our ministerial imagination so that our lives might both be informed by it, and become one with it.

I have sought to place Rublev's classic icon before the many groups with which I have been privileged to work, suggesting that our unceasing focus on this central Christian experience offers us not only a sure path of orthodoxy in faith but also, most significantly, the most steady means of acting rightly in ministry. Our ministry, both in content and in style, finds its definition, its origin and its orientation within the heart of this extraordinary Mystery of beauty, truth and

---

1   See Declan Marmion and Gesa Thiessan, 'The Revival of Trinitarian Theology,' in *Trinity and Salvation: Theological, spiritual and aesthetic perspectives*, edited by Declan Marmion and Gesa Thiessen. Studies in Theology, Society and Culture Vol. 2, (Oxford et al: Peter Lang, 2009), 1.

2   For a full treatment on the icon, see Gabriel Bunge, *The Rublev Trinity: The icon of the Trinity by the monk-painter Andrei Rublev*, translated by Andrew Louth, (Crestwood, New York: St. Vladimir's Seminary Press, 2007).

life. The reflections that follow seek to integrate this conviction with the contemporary experience of ministry along with key insights into the Trinitarian mystery afforded by the Reformed theologian, Jürgen Moltmann whose writings I have greatly valued in my own spiritual journey.[3]

In bringing these reflections now to publication I am grateful to those retreatants with whom I first shared them: the clergy of the Australian dioceses of Newcastle-Maitland, Lismore, Geraldton, Rockhampton, Bunbury, Townsville, Port Pirie, and Brisbane, the students, priests and brothers of the Australian Province of the Society of the Divine Word, and the many parishes and groups of Religious throughout Australia with whom I have shared this imagination.

I am grateful to the editor of *The Furrow*, Ronan Drury, for the several opportunities to publish parts of this publication in the past, particularly as 'The Trinity: Source of Ministry', *The Furrow* 56 (May, 2005), 284-292 and 'The Heart of Mercy', *The Furrow* 60 (December 2009), 681-685. My gratitude also goes to Ms Margaret Watts of the Veech Library of the Catholic Institute of Sydney for her uncanny ability to track the sources of a number of the references in the publication. My thanks is extended also to Fr Michael Goonan, and St Pauls Publications in Australia, for bringing these reflections to print and for the support in this regard provided by the President of the Catholic Institute of Sydney, Dr Gerard Kelly, Bishop David Walker of the Diocese of Broken Bay, and the Australian Provincial of the Society of the Divine Word Missionaries, Fr Tim Norton.

---

3   The works of Moltmann that I am indebted to for my reflections on the Trinity are *The Crucified God* (London: SCM Press, 1974), *The Power of the Powerless: The word of liberation for today* (San Francisco: Harper and Row, Publishers, 1983); *The Trinity and the Kingdom: The doctrine of God*, translated by Margaret Kohl, (San Francisco: Harper, 1991); *History and the Triune God: Contributions to Trinitarian theology* (New York: Crossroad, 1992); and *The Spirit of Life: A universal affirmation* (Minneapolis: Fortress Press, 1992). For other very helpful treatments of Trinitarian theology today see Anne Hunt, *Trinity* (Maryknoll, NY: Orbis Books, 2005) and Neil Ormerod, *The Trinity: Retrieving the Western Tradition* (Milwaukee: Marquette University Press, 2005).

CHAPTER ONE

WATCHFUL AND WAITING

It is a time of concern for those exercising ministry in the Church, both personally and pastorally. For many priests, as one instance, it is a time of painful uncertainty and re-adjustment as they discover themselves more and more within a community of ministries whilst they seek, nonetheless, to affirm the indispensable place of their sacramental identity. For those who participate in the many new forms of ecclesial ministry which now exist there are those many challenges of formation, and the frustration of exercising leadership in complex circumstances both within the Church and in society.

As the following encounter that the disciples have with Jesus dramatically illustrates, though, Christ comes to us not apart from such concern but in the midst of such anxiety.

> It happened one day he got into a boat with his disciples and said to them, 'Let us cross over to the other side of the lake.' So they set out, and as they sailed he fell asleep. When a squall of wind came down on the lake the boat started shipping water and they found themselves in danger. So they went to rouse him saying, 'Master! Master! We are lost!' Then he woke up and rebuked the wind and the rough water; and they subsided and it was calm again. He said to them, 'Where is your faith?' They were awestruck, and astounded and said to one another, 'Who can this be, that gives orders even to winds and waves and they obey him' (*Lk* 8: 22-25).

The peace that we desire as ministers of the gospel in the midst of all the challenges that swirl around us does not come to us in any genuine way other than through the crucible of such stormy experience. In the Spirit we must stand in the face of the storm and discover the approach of the Lord there, and not in another place. Some years ago, the English writer, John F. X. Harriot expressed this spiritual imperative by remarking,

Much modern spiritual writing, it seems to me, holds out a false ideal of wholeness and happiness, as if we could on this earth anticipate the blessedness of heaven and that something is seriously wrong if we don't. But though some Christians may be called to be neat and clean and well-advised, others may have to glorify God as slobs, freaks, duffers and muddlers of every kind and variety. As the psychotherapists love to say, 'The physician heals by his own wound,' and perhaps for many of us our inadequacy is the only road to wisdom and charity, the most healthy outlook one that accepts our own unhealthiness, the best way of making the most of life a tough-minded recognition that much of it is tough. Peace in the Christian scheme of things is not a comfortable absence of conflict and stress. We have to pluck tranquility out of pain and suffering, tension and confusion, learn to hear in the heart of the storm the voice that says, 'Peace, it is I.'[1]

I suspect that many of us who exercise ministry today could well identify with Harriot's spiritual observation. We too often feel overwhelmed, inadequate to the tasks that relentlessly impact upon us. There is a part of us that would like to simply have these winds and currents subside so that we could once again live out our ministry in an untrammeled kind of way. The Spirit of the risen Christ, however, does not allow us the luxury of stepping away from our concern but rather impels us to step into it. It is here in the midst of the storm of our concern, and not apart from it, that the Spirit offers us peace. This is not the peace that is the absence of concern but a peace that takes us through our concern to the deepest sources of both the truth of God and of ourselves, a place of both surrender and reception. There we find the still small voice which is the bedrock of our identity in ministry, which holds us firm and enables us with courage. 'Peace I leave with you; my peace I give you' (*Jn* 14:27). Peace is the gentle invitation held out to us in the midst of the storm.

---

1   John. F. X. Harriot, 'The Aspirin Society', *The Tablet* (17 March 1990), 334.

But what is the peace of Christ? What is our peace as ministers of the gospel? However we might seek to answer this, the peace born of both surrender and reception must first be listened for.

I am reminded of an old African parable about how best to catch a lion. When looking for a lion never go hunting for it, says the parable. The lion will always elude you. To catch a lion it is necessary to stop still, to light a fire and to wait for the lion to find you. In many ways, the parable is a good description of our relationship with God and presents us with the key to that new experience of peace for which we long as ministers. Like the African warrior we need to learn that a too concentrated search for God – and ourselves for that matter – can only amplify frustration. We have to discover, sometimes not without a struggle, that it is God who finds us. Along the way we learn to trust this. This faith is deepened by our Christian recognition that the Mystery in which we are embraced, as it is disclosed to us in the experience of Jesus, is one of unparalleled intimacy, of gracious hospitality. The Mystery desires us and seeks us out. Like the African warrior, our task is to live in expectancy, in sensitivity, to the Divine Lion's approach, aware of the many indicators that signal the Mystery's immanence and invitation.

In our confusion and anxiety we can think that it is imperative to regain a sense of control. We can be like the Masai elder who initially thought for a person really to believe,

> is like a lion going after its prey. His nose and eyes and ears pick up the prey. His legs give him the speed to catch it. All the power of his body is involved in the terrible death leap and single blow to the neck with the front paw . . . And as the animal goes down the lion envelops it in his arms (Africans refer to the front legs of an animal as its arms) pulls it to himself, and makes it part of himself. This is the way a lion kills. This is the way a man believes. This is what faith is.[2]

---

2   Vincent J. Donovan, *Christianity Rediscovered: An epistle from the Masai* (London: SCM Press, 1978), 63.

However, the Masai elder moves with wise agility beyond this initial consideration. 'I looked at the elder in silence and amazement. …But my wise old teacher was not finished yet,' recounts Donovan:

> 'We did not search you, out, Padri [sic],' he said to me. 'We did not even want you to come to us. You searched us out. You followed us away from your house into the bush, into the hills, into the plains, into the steppes where our cattle are, into the hills where we take our cattle for water, into our villages, into our homes. You told us of the High God, how we must search for him, even leave our land and our people to find him. But we have not done this. We have not left our land. We have not searched for him. He has searched for us. He has searched *us* out and found us.' All the time we think we are the lion. In the end, the lion is God.[3]

Waiting for the Divine Lion, we are to listen. Listening is a simple skill but one of the most difficult for us to practice. Perhaps, precisely because of its simplicity, we keep forgetting the significance of listening in Christian discipleship generally, and in ministerial life, particularly. Yet, with the attentiveness, the vigilance, the mindfulness of the African warrior, we recognise the potential occasioned by listening that Jean Pierre de Caussade identified in the eighteenth century when he wrote,

> Faith sees the work of divine action in everything. It sees that Jesus Christ lives in all things, extending his influence over the centuries so that the briefest moment and the tiniest atom contain a portion of that hidden life and its mysterious work. Jesus Christ, after his resurrection, surprised the disciples when he appeared before them in disguise . . . the same Jesus still lives and works among us, still surprises . . . there is no moment when God is not manifest . . . Everything that happens to us, in us, and through us, embraces and conceals God's divine but veiled purpose . . . If we could pierce that veil and if we were vigilant and attentive, God would unceasingly reveal himself to us and we would rejoice in his works and in all that happens to us we would say to everything, 'It is the Lord!'[4]

---

3   Donovan, *Christianity Rediscovered*, 63.

4   Jean Pierre de Caussade, *The Sacrament of the Present Moment* (London: Collins Fount, 1981), 106.

In our own time the challenge is the same. It is to be ready to perceive even in the midst of our own concern and confusion the approach of the Lord. In our listening we are waiting to be struck by his word. 'Speak to us a word,' the disciples in the desert would say to their spiritual father. Not just any word, but a word that strikes us, a word that changes the way in which we see ourselves. They prayed for the gift of compunction, the experience of being 'pierced through' by a word – a word which would enable them to recognise what little distance they had come on the spiritual journey and to what lengths they were being invited into the life of God.

Like the African warrior we are sitting at our campfire, still, watching. What will this word be? In our waiting a word will come to us. It will not just be any word but one that will open something up for us. It will be a word of invitation and of promise:

> For I know the plans I have for you . . . plans to prosper you and not to harm you, plans to give you hope and a future. Then you will call on me and come and pray to me, and I will listen to you. You will seek me and find me when you seek me with all your heart. I will be found by you . . . and bring you back from captivity (*Jer* 29: 11-14).

Throughout I have been emphasizing, however, that this word of promise and invitation comes to us in the midst of, and not apart from, the questions that swirl around us at this time. Indeed, it is the questions that challenge us to be particularly watchful, attentive, mindful, listening. We live in a period in which the call in particular is to listen.

In this particular Advent period in history, stretching forward beyond the opening years of this new millennium, as ministers in the Church we are to first and foremost listen again. The discernment, however, about what the Spirit might be saying to the Churches at this time must be undertaken in the light of the central mystery of our faith. This is the mystery of the Trinity.

We are challenged at this unique time in our story to reflect on the mystery of the Trinity and to ask what this might mean for us as those exercising ministry. To extend the metaphor of the African parable, this is *the* story that we are to tell around our own campfire in our waiting and watchfulness. As we tell this story again and again, as we deepen our appreciation of this central story of our Christian identity, we might discover our ministerial identity anew. And precisely in the celebration of the story, we are made even more watchful, vigilant, expectant, full of anticipation. As we listen anew, that word of peace for which we long might then begin to disclose itself to us in an unimagined way. How can our renewed appreciation of the Mystery impact on our style of ministry at this time? And what does this Mystery mean for our world? How does this understanding of God that we have as Christian ministers change the way we see things and do things? What does it offer a hungry world?

CHAPTER TWO

A TRINITARIAN MINISTRY

The architect of the gargantuan Parliament building in Canberra, Australia, Romaldo Guirgola, apparently was fond of saying 'great buildings begin with great ideas.' In other words, if you can't imagine the possibilities first, the end result will not be all that significant. Great buildings begin with great ideas. If great buildings begin in great ideas, great lives, too, begin with great images.

The topic of images and imagination can, at first, present with some apprehension. We can confuse both with fantasy, with 'make believe'. A more accurate understanding of imagination, however, reminds us that imagination is the faculty which renders something possible because of the disclosive images that it creates. Thus, there exists a fundamental link between our imagination and our behaviour. The way in which we imagine something determines the way we act. This is particularly the case when it comes to what might be termed 'operative images' fashioned by our imagination.[1] 'Operative images' are those images that especially determine the way in which we see ourselves and our world and which, therefore, allow certain possibilities and disallow other ones. Let us not forget Rainer Maria Rilke's advice to the young Mr Kappus when he said,

> *Everything* is in gestation and then bringing forth. To let each impression and each germ of a feeling come to completion quite in itself, in the dark, in the expressible, the unconscious, beyond the reach of one's own understanding, and await with deep humility and patience the birth-hour of a new clarity: that alone is living the artist's life – in understanding as in work.[2] [Italics in original]

---

1   For a fuller exploration of this theme, see Richard. T. Knowles 'Fantasy and Imagination' in Imagination, Memory and Anticipation in Human and Christian Formation, *Studies in Formative Spirituality*, Vol 6 (February 1985), 53-64.

2   Rainer Maria Rilke, 'Letter to Mr. Kappus, 23 April 1903,' in *Letters to a Young Poet*, translated by M.D. Herter Norton, (New York: W.W. Norton & Company, Inc., 1934), 27-28.

And later to the same budding poet,

> Think, dear sir, of the world that you carry within you, and call
> this thinking what you will; whether it be remembering your
> own childhood or yearning towards your own future – only be
> attentive to that which rises up in you and set it above everything
> that you observe about you.[3]

Our 'self-image' is a clear 'operative image'. We are familiar with its implications. However, our 'God image' is, likewise, an 'operative image'. The way in which we imagine God determines an entire framework of behaviour and is, perhaps, even more significant than our 'self-image' since the latter is, in many ways, itself, determined by our 'God image'. Certainly, our way of praying and the way in which we see the world itself will be a direct consequence of our 'God image.' Further, the process of conversion represents a deepening of our imagination about God, letting go of images inadequate to our widening experience, and conforming our images more faithfully to what we are offered in and through Jesus. In the process of a developing faith we are called to confront what images of God we actually do bear, whatever our declared rhetoric, and test them as the letter of St John urges us to do with the spirits generally (cf. *1 Jn* 4: 1). Cardinal Martini, formerly of Milan, has described conversion, itself, as a change in our image of God.

At different times along our spiritual journey we are forced to confront the images of God that we carry. Life questions those images, undoes them and opens us out into a new imagination about God. In this creating and undoing of the way we think about God, Jesus comes towards us and invites us to consider a whole new way of thinking about God – a way of thinking about God that we could never have, if left to ourselves. He leads us into a deeper and deeper, a richer and richer, understanding of God. He invites us to let go of our inadequate images of God and to grow into his own imagination about God, into his own very experience of God. It is as if he says to us, 'Let go

---

3   Rilke, 'Letter to Mr. Kappus, 23 December 1903,' in *Letters to a Young Poet*, 46.

of the small imagination you have of God, and receive a new way of imagining God that will change your life! Your own experience of God is too small, too influenced in so many unhelpful ways. Let it go, and grow into mine. This is my gift to you.'

Thus, we grow out of our own poor images of God, and we grow into the image of God that Jesus himself has. We are given the imagination of Jesus. This is his gift to us. John O'Donohue, the late Irish writer, speaks of this gift:

> Jesus had a wonderful depth of sensibility and imagination. All his language is fresh and alert. It is a language full of thresholds; it opens the heart to the eternal. It took a powerfully disciplined and inspired imagination to discover and articulate the presence and shape of the Trinity. No other shape of deity holds such power and tension. In the Trinity the pure wildness of the unknown surges within the intimacy of personal form. . . It is no wonder that William Blake called Christ the Imagination.[4]

Jesus opens out for a whole new way of understanding God – a God who is pure relationship, a God of infinite communion, a God who is a community of persons in relationship. Our God is a divine community of persons: a mystery of persons in relationship in which each Person is defined by the other, with the other, in the other, for the other, through the other, to the other. It is a mystery of communion, a circle of life, of understanding and of love; a mystery of mutual self-emptying become self-giving, eternal giving and receiving, infinite loving and being loved, desiring and desired; a mystery of infinite hospitality, an eternal banquet inviting us to its feast – a circular dance sweeping us up into its rhythm of relationality as Hippolytus of Rome in the second century described.

> O thou leader of the mystic round-dance! O divine Pasch and new feast of all things! O cosmic festal gathering! O joy of the universe, honour, ecstasy, exquisite delight by which dark death

---

4   John O'Donohue, 'The Priestliness of the Human Heart,' *The Way Supplement* 83 (Summer 1995), 51.

is destroyed . . . and the people that were in the depths arise from the dead and announce to all the hosts of heaven: 'The thronging choir from earth is coming home.'[5]

To take our gaze off this mystery is to lay ourselves open to the possibility of distortion, not just in our orthodoxy, but importantly, also in our orthopraxis – the way in which we act rightly. It is difficult to remain faithful to his imagination for it is demanding. Writing on priestly ministry, in particular, Pope John Paul II was very clear, however, that,

> the nature and mission of the ministerial priesthood cannot be defined except through this multiple and rich interconnection of relationships which arise from the Blessed Trinity and are prolonged in the communion of the Church, as a sign and instrument of Christ, of communion with God and of the unity of all humanity. It is within the Church's mystery, as a mystery of Trinitarian communion in missionary tension, that every Christian identity is revealed and likewise the identity of the priest and his ministry . . .[6]

Though the Pope was addressing ordained ministry in such a statement, the insight holds true for all ministries in the Church. In the Trinity, we discover ourselves anew as men and women of both communion and mission. We give form to this central mystery of our Christian faith, representing as *personae ecclesiae* the truth that, as Dennis Edwards wrote, 'The Church is the sacrament of relationships, called to witness to the relational God at the heart of the universe. This is the grace that the Church is for the world. It is a grace for all ages, but one desperately important in our own.'[7]

---

5   See Hippolytus, *Homiliae in Pascha*, 6 [G 59, 744D, f.], quoted in Hugo Rahner, *Man at Play: Or did you ever practice eutrapelia?*, translated by Brian Battershaw and Edward Quinn, (London: Burns & Oates, 1965), 86. Hippolytus also refers to the cosmic circular dance in his *Refutation of All Heresies*, Book V, ch. 21. For the images of God as dance in early Christian literature see also Ronald Gagne, Thomas Kane and Robert VerEecke, *Introducing Dance in Christian Worship*, (Washington, D.C.: The Pastoral Press, 1984), 38-41.

6   John Paul II, *Pastores dabo vobis*, Apostolic Exhortation on the Formation of Priests in the Circumstances of the Present Day, (25 March, 1992), n.12

7   Dennis Edwards, 'The Church as Sacrament of Relationships,' *Pacifica* 8 (1995), 195.

As sacrament of this extraordinary Mystery, ecclesial life needs to be characterised by attentive listening to each other and open conversation; in a tension which respects both unity and diversity – never one at the expense of the other; through a variety of charisms which work in collaboration with each other; in a deep concern for inclusiveness and reconciliation. We cannot honour this God and act in ways that are not collaborative, dialogical and inclusive or in ways that are not reconciling, healing and thoroughly relational. To be a Church sacramental of this Mystery means that we both share in and co-operate with God's own dream that the whole of creation be gathered up into this same experience of communion, in which nothing is excluded.

As Moltmann declares, the Trinity is our social program.[8] It is not an abstract doctrine but a way of living together. We cannot worship this God and act in ways of conquest, domination, and lordship. But neither can this God be reverenced without becoming deeply sensitive to where and how the pain of exclusion might be being experienced in the world. Consequently, our understanding of God as Communion means that must work to redress the experience of exclusion. In our ministry hell is transformed into heaven for hell is isolation in its extreme, heaven is communion in its fullness. In so doing we give practical expression to that fundamental link between communion and mission expressed by John Paul II:

> Communion and mission are profoundly connected with each other, they interpenetrate and mutually imply each other, to the point that communion represents both the source and the fruit of mission: communion gives rise to mission and mission is accomplished in communion.[9]

Because of its source ministerial life is to be marked by both communion and mission, as is the Triune life itself. Responsible for,

---

8   This is a theme developed at length by Jürgen Moltmann, *The Trinity and the Kingdom: The doctrine of God*, translated by Margaret Kohl, (San Francisco: Harper, 1991).

9   *Christifidelis laici*, 'On the Vocation and Mission of the Lay Faithful in the World', Post-Synodal Apostolic Exhortation (30 December 1988), n. 32.

and contributing to the life of communities, we are to be men and women of communion[10] It is this commitment to communion which gives rise to a new experience of mission. Our mission is to share our experience of communion with others. Our mission is to enable others to experience the invitation to communion so that they might be drawn into the Communion of God's own life.

Christian ministry is therefore at the service of the creation and the sustaining of a community marked by Trinitarian qualities and at the service of fostering ever widening circles of that community's relationships. As ministers of the *communio*, we are to be agents of participation, collaboration and reconciliation forging a unity in the midst, but not at the expense of, diversity. As ministers of *missio* Christian ministers are to be agents of hospitality, embrace an ex-centricity that in particular addresses the places of isolation, marginalisation and exclusion as they are represented in whatever context the Christian discovers themselves to be.

The Trinity – and its strategy-in-action, the Kingdom – presents us with the template for all pastoral planning, for all congregational decision making about ministry. It places before us the abiding questions: 'Where does the ethic of accumulation, fear, selfishness and judgment work in such a way to exclude, marginalise and isolate?'[11] 'How might we respond, as a community, to those places in such a way as to transform the experience of exclusion into one of embrace?'[12] These questions will be answered differently according to context which is an ever-changing reality. It is our readiness to discern the changing character of the answer that gives account of our fidelity to the Mission of which our ministry shall always remain in service.

---

10   Cf. *Pastores dabo vobis*, n. 43.

11   This ethic as compared to the messianic practice of Jesus is treated in Hugo Echegaray, *The Practice of Jesus*, translated from the Spanish by Matthew J. O'Connell, (Maryknoll, New York: Orbis Books/Melbourne, Australia: Dove Communications, 1984), 93-97.

12   See Miroslav Volf, *Exclusion and Embrace: A theological exploration of identity, otherness, and reconciliation*. (Nashville: Abingdon Press, 1996).

Understanding Christian ministry as effecting both *communio* and *mission* – in dynamic tension with each other – fundamentally renders it entirely 'relational.' Throughout *Pastores dabo vobis*, John Paul II refers to this intrinsic quality of Christian ministry – and priesthood particularly,

> The priest should be able to know the depths of the human heart, to perceive difficulties and problems, to make meeting and dialogue easy, to create trust and co-operation . . . of special importance is the capacity to relate to others. This is truly fundamental for a person who is called to be responsible for a community and to be a 'man of communion.'[13]

Whether we are ordained or otherwise, however, in our diverse ministries we are all bearers of the mission of the Triune life which desires that all of creation be brought out of isolation and fragmentation into the experience of communion and wholeness. In this radical integration between communion and mission, ministry is rendered with an intrinsically relational character. Ministry that is relational in its very dynamism is bread to a hungry world in which relationship is under such stress. Statistics on the breakdown in relationships, the emergence of revocable relationships, the drop in free-associations, the rise of depression and suicide, especially amongst our youth, and the reliance on 'relationship substitutes' are evidence of this stress. It is an urgent pastoral consideration to imagine new forms of the experience of community in which people can experience a quality of relationship from which alone come identity, dignity and future.

It is worth noting here in this regard that for those of us who might exercise our ministry as celibates this constitutive relational element of ministry implies a particular imagination about the practice of celibacy in particular. The Trinity mirrors the possibility of a vital celibate commitment as one that is entirely directed to the cultivation of relationship. Since the Trinity discloses that we are made for

---

13 *Pastores dabo vobis*, n. 43.

relationship we are able to situate our sexuality primarily as the instinct for relationship. It is not without significance that, at least from a male perspective, the more isolated one is the greater the genital tension and the more relational we are the more natural becomes genital integration. Christian celibacy, which will always find its true home in the practice of community, is not a choice to be in relationship or otherwise. Rather, it is a choice to be in relationship but according to a particular manner. Christian celibacy is the choice for a community of relationships in the recognition that it is in this network of relationships that celibates become most fully themselves. From a Triune basis, I think we can, in some ways, imagine celibacy as 'the sacrament of hospitality.' The more relational the practice of celibacy is characterised, the more it is truly able to give witness to, and make present, the hospitality of the communion that is God.

Though the practice of hospitality expresses the deeper possibilities in celibate living, specifically, I believe mission itself, generally, can be imagined through the lens of this ancient Christian value. Christian ministry is an exercise of hospitality, a reflection of the hospitality that characterises the divine life. As the Triune God speaks of a profound hospitality, so, too, Christian ministry is called to be transparent of this. Hospitality always tends towards communion. It calls forth an effort to be open to that which is closed, to enlarge what is tight and narrow, to re-establish communication between persons in such a manner that the life of God can flow and circulate. As one of the three movements of the spiritual life as identified by Henri Nouwen, hospitality is the journey by which the stranger becomes a friend rather than an enemy. Who are the strangers we come across in our life and ministry? Who are the permanent strangers in our community? These are the people with whom Christian ministry, sourced in the Triune God, is particularly concerned. As ministers of communion, our heart of hospitality leads us to being deeply attentive to the stranger; our hearts are open to the possibility that the stranger might bear blessing. Of course, in the exercise of hospitality it is we who are enriched. 'Do not forget to show hospitality to strangers, for by doing so some people have shown hospitality to angels without knowing it' (*Heb* 13:2; cf. *Gen* 18). Ultimately, it is Jesus himself who is welcomed in hospitality to the stranger (cf. *Rev* 3:20, *Mt* 25:36-40; *Jn* 13:20). Thus being the ones who are blessed – and evangelised – in our encounter with strangeness, a key criterion of discernment begins to present itself in the life of ministry: are we the ones who are changed by our ministry?

The imagination of God as Trinity, this image of God given to us by and through Jesus, calls us into a life that is relational, hospitable and, by extension, deeply conversational. When we live this way, according to the image of the Trinity impressed deep within our being, we live a gracious life, a life filled with grace. The African notion of *Ubuntu* has a good deal to teach us about such a life. What is *Ubuntu*? Desmond Tutu of South Africa defines it in this way:

> In my culture and tradition the highest praise that can be given to someone is . . an acknowledgement that he or she has this wonderful quality, *ubuntu*. It is a reference to their actions towards their fellow human beings; it has to do with how they regard people and how they see themselves within their intimate relationships, their familial relationships and within the broader community. *Ubuntu* addresses a central tenet of African philosophy: the essence of what it is to be human.

> The definition of this concept has two parts. The first is that the person is friendly, hospitable, generous, caring and compassionate. In other words, someone who will use their strengths on behalf of others – the weak and the poor and the ill – and not take advantage of anyone. This person treats others as he or she would be treated. And because of this they express the second part of the concept which concerns openness, large-heartedness. They share their worth. In so doing, their humanity is recognised and becomes inextricably bound to theirs.

> People with *ubuntu* are approachable and welcoming, their attitude is kindly and well disposed, they are not threatened by

the goodness in others because their own esteem and self-worth is generated by knowing they belong to a greater whole. To recast the Cartesian proposition 'I think, therefore I am', *ubuntu* would phrase it, 'I am human because I belong'. Put another way, 'a person is a person through other people' . . . [14]

Ubuntu runs on the principle that if I diminish you, I diminish myself. Elsewhere Desmond Tutu remarks, 'We think of ourselves far too frequently as just individuals, separated from one another, whereas you are connected and what you do affects the whole world. When you do well, it spreads out; it is for the whole of humanity.'[15] Likewise, Nelson Mandela himself talks about this notion of *Ubuntu*. He recounts how it operates through the hospitality we offer one another:

A traveler through a country would stop at a village and he didn't have to ask for food or for water. Once he stops, the people give him food, entertain him. That is one aspect of *Ubuntu* but it will have various aspects. *Ubuntu* does not mean that people should not address [their own needs]. The question . . . is: Are you going to do so in order to enable the community around you to be able to improve?[1]

As we gaze upon the Trinity and as we are drawn into this Divine Circle of Life let us commit ourselves to this quality of *Ubuntu*. If our actions in ministry are characterised through and through with this quality then the ministry which emerges will be one of love, a ministry which bears the imprint of the Trinity, a ministry which becomes a living icon of the Mystery of the Trinity.

---

14   Desmond Tutu, 'Introduction,' in Ubuntu, *Compassion: The words and inspiration of the Dalia Lama* (Sydney: Hachette Australia, 2008).

15   Desmond Tutu, Speech, 2008, cited on 'Ubuntu,' http://en.wikipedia.org/wiki/Ubuntu_(philosophy)

CHAPTER THREE

HEARTS SHAPED BY THE WORD WHO IS JESUS

The Son is the image of the invisible God, the firstborn over all creation. For in him all things were created: things in heaven and on earth, visible and invisible, whether thrones or powers or rulers or authorities; all things have been created through him and for him. He is before all things, and in him all things hold together. And he is the head of the body, the church; he is the beginning and the firstborn from among the dead, so that in everything he might have the supremacy. For God was pleased to have all his fullness dwell in him, and through him to reconcile to himself all things, whether things on earth or things in heaven, by making peace through his blood, shed on the cross.

(*Col* 1: 15-20)

As we gaze upon Rublev's icon of the Trinity our attention is drawn immediately to the central figure, the figure of Christ. Indeed we never take our gaze off the person of Jesus. Our spirituality is always Christocentric, and only because it is Christocentric, does it become Trinitarian. It is our sustained gaze on Christ which opens out for us this wider, broader experience of God as Trinity. This occurs, however, *whilst* we keep our gaze on Christ; we never take our gaze off him. All we have comes through our encounter with the person of Jesus.

How might the abiding focus on the Son be illustrated? Let me share a story about another son once sent to me by someone:

> Years ago, there was a very wealthy man who, with his devoted young son, shared a passion for art collecting. Together they travelled around the world, adding only the finest art treasures to their collection. Priceless works by Picasso, van Gogh, Monet and many others adorned the walls of the family estate.

The widowed elder man looked on with satisfaction as his only child became an experienced art collector. The son's trained eye and sharp business mind caused his father to beam with pride as they dealt with art collectors around the world.

As winter approached, war engulfed the nation, and the young man left to serve his country. After only a few short weeks, his father received a telegram. His beloved son was missing in action. The art collector anxiously awaited more news, fearing he would never see his son again. Within days, his fears were confirmed. The young man had died while rushing to a fellow soldier as a medic.

Distraught and lonely, the old man faced the upcoming Christmas holidays with anguish and sadness. The joy of the season, a season that he and his son had so looked forward to, would visit his house no longer. On Christmas morning, a knock on the door awakened the depressed old man.

As he walked to the door, the masterpieces of art on the walls only reminded him that his son was not coming home. As he opened the door, he was greeted by a soldier with a large package in his hand. He introduced himself to the man saying, 'I was a friend of your son. I was the one he was rescuing when he died. May I come inside for a few moments? I have something to show you.'

As the two began to talk, the soldier told of how the man's son had told everyone of his father's love of fine art. 'I'm an artist,' said the soldier, 'and I want to give you this.' As the old man unwrapped the package, the paper gave way to reveal a portrait of the man's son. Though the world would never consider it the work of a genius, the painting featured the young man's face in striking detail. Overcome with emotion, the man thanked the soldier, promising to hang the picture above the fireplace. A few hours later, after the soldier had departed, the old man set about his task.

True to his word, the painting went above the fireplace, pushing aside thousands of dollars of paintings. And then the man sat in his chair and spent Christmas gazing at the gift he had been given. During the days and weeks that followed, the man realised that even though his son was no longer with him, the boy's life would live on because of those he had touched. He would soon learn that his son had rescued dozens of wounded soldiers before a bullet stilled his caring heart.

As the stories of the son's gallantry continued to reach him, fatherly pride and satisfaction began to ease the grief. The painting of his son soon became his most prized possession, far eclipsing any interest in the pieces for which museums around the round clamored. He told his neighbors it was the greatest gift he had ever received.

The following spring, the old man became ill and passed away. The art world was in anticipation. With the collector's passing, and his only son dead, those paintings would be sold at auction. According to the will of the old man, all of the art works would be auctioned on Christmas day, the day he had received his greatest gift.

The day soon arrived and art collectors from around the world gathered to bid on some of the world's most spectacular paintings. Dreams would be fulfilled this day; greatness would be achieved as many would claim, 'I have the greatest collection.' The auction began with a painting not on any museum's lists. It was the painting of the man's son. The auctioneer asked for an opening bid. 'Who will open the bidding with $100?' he asked. Minutes passed. No one spoke. The room was silent. Minutes passed. From the back of the room came, 'Who cares about that painting? It's just a picture of his son. Let's forget it and go on to the good stuff.' More voices echoed in agreement. 'No we have to sell this one first,' replied the auctioneer.

'Now, who will take the son?' Finally, a friend of the old man spoke. 'Will you take ten dollars for the painting. That is all I have. I knew the boy and would like to have it.' 'I have ten dollars. Will anyone go higher?' called the auctioneer. After more silence, the auctioneer said, 'Going once, going twice, gone.' The gavel fell. Cheers filled the room and someone exclaimed, 'Now we can get on with it and we can bid on these treasures!'

The auctioneer looked at the audience and announced the auction was over. Stunned disbelief quieted the room. Someone spoke up and asked, 'What do you mean it's over? We didn't come here for a picture of some old guy's son. What about all of these paintings? There are millions of dollars of art here! I demand you explain what's going on here!' The auctioneer replied, 'It's very simple. According to the will of the father, whoever takes the son . . . gets it all.'

We have been given a Word. And that Word is Jesus, the only Son of the Father. In accord with the insight of John of the Cross, God has only ever said one word: Jesus. 'The Father spoke one Word, which was his Son, and this Word He always speaks in eternal silence, and in silence must it be heard by the soul.'[1] 'Jesus' is the one Word uttered by the Father, the one Word in and through which all creation has its being, as the prologue to the Gospel of John reminds us.

Since everything is contained in this one single Word, nothing more needs to be said! All that we need to hear has been proclaimed! It is a word which changes the way in which we see our life and which changes the way in which we do things. It is the single word which reminds us deep in our hearts that forgiveness is stronger than vengeance, that love is more enduring than hatred, that hope is brighter than despair, that life is stronger than death. It is a word that opens up for us new possibility even in the midst of what might be extraordinary limitation.

It is the Word for which we are listening by the campfire we have lit, watchful and waiting. It is by the constant, sustained reflection on this Word, disclosed in the narrative and teaching of the Scripture, that we hear what God wishes us to hear, what God wishes to reveal to us, what

---

1   John of the Cross, *Maxims on Love*, n.21, in *The Collected Works of St. John of the Cross*, translated by Kieran Kavanaugh and Otilio Rodriguez, (London: Thomas Nelson, 1964), 675.

God wants to communicate to us about God's own self and indeed about ourselves. The echoes of this Word continue to reverberate through time and history, in our own context and story. It is the task of the praying Christian to listen for the reverberations of the Word for where and how they occur.

As we receive the Word who is Jesus ever more deeply in our life we set our hearts on the one thing necessary, the Kingdom into which he is leading us. In our ministry, we have become disciples of the Kingdom. Yet, setting our hearts on the one thing necessary involves a necessary renunciation. There is a certain 'rupture' in discipleship, a certain 'death'. We see this in Mark 1:16-20 in the call of the first disciples (Mk 1:16-20) and in the account of Jesus' encounter with the rich young man (Matt 19:16-22). Though it is Jesus who comes in search of us, and who finds us where we are, we are not simply left where we are by his discovery. He calls us to follow him. We are called from one place to another, even within ourselves.

This movement, though, is not an automatic one. As Rublev's icon depicts we are given a cup to drink. To become a disciple of the Kingdom we must take this cup, the cup that is the passion of Jesus. We are led into the passion of Jesus symbolised both by the cup of sacrifice placed in Rublev's icon on the centre of the table in front of Jesus, and by the wood of the tree behind the figure of Jesus, the Cross.

Passion is a word with many different meanings. Pierre Wolff remarks about the word, 'passion':

> In the context of the Christian liturgy, the word signifies sufferings, dereliction, and death. It implies everything that Jesus experienced during those days: betrayal and denial, rejection and abandonment, and other ordeals. The word 'passion' in this context suggests little that is pleasant for a human being.

> [However], we often forget that we use it is an adjective when we speak of a passionate love. This time the word has a very positive connotation: it means that what we describe is pushed to its

very limits, to its fulfillment. When we see a passionate love, we sometimes talk about the madness of love.

That is what the Passion of Jesus Christ is about. As Christians, don't we see in these events a passion-tide of love in human flesh, the crashing waves of God called Love by John (1 John 4:8)? So when we read or pray the Passion narrative, we listen to a love story – not a romance, but the story of God's love for us, the story of God as Love.[2]

In our ministry we enter into the Lord's passion – in this sense, we become passionate in life – about life – as he was. Each of us in our ministry is called to become a passionate person. In this sense we can never have enough passion. William McNamara lamented once that there was not enough passion in our Church. He said,

Married lovers are . . . not passionate enough. And what's more, neither are celibate lovers, who should be at least as . . . passionate as married people. There is no other way to be a really great lover. And if . . . men and women are not great lovers, what hope is there for Christianity?[3]

Our discipleship of the crucified and risen Lord, the passionate One, calls us into lives of greater love. The story of Jesus' passion into which we are being drawn discloses to us, however, the true meaning of love: a self-emptying become a self-giving.

As Jesus leads us onwards to a deeper life, above all he calls us to let go of that which inhibits our freedom to follow him in such a self-emptying become a self-giving. In our ministry we have to let go of the illusions we have of ourselves, our self-protective instincts, (Mt 10:37-39). When he calls, love leaves fear behind (Mk 1:16-20; Mt 19:16-22). As Pope Benedict XVI teaches us, this is the meaning of love:

Love is indeed 'ecstasy', not in the sense of a moment of intoxication, but rather as a journey, an ongoing exodus out of

---

2   Pierre Wolff, *God's Passion our Passion* (Ligouri, Missouri: Triumph Books, 1994), 5-6

3   William McNamara, *Mystical Passion* (Mahwah, New Jersey: Paulist Press, 1977), 3

the closed inward-looking self towards its liberation through self-giving, and thus towards authentic self-discovery and indeed the discovery of God: 'Whoever seeks to gain his life will lose it, but whoever loses his life will preserve it' (*Lk* 17: 33).[4]

Another contemporary writer expresses it this way that living the Christian mystery is about how 'we move on in our lives from what is deadly to what is life-giving, from what is selfish to what is gracious, from what is shadowed to what is luminous.'[5] In this way, we are never to dry off from our baptism, according to Gerard Baumbach, that is we are always entering into the waters of the Lord's death and rising with him to newness of life.[6]

This, however, is not something dramatic and full of display:

> What we must at all costs not do is imagine our participation in the cross or dream of the extraordinary. The real acceptance of death today for each of us is our disposition to do completely the will of the Father, as Jesus did. The death to be accepted is first of all death to that in us which is an obstacle to trust in God and others, an obstacle to fraternal service and giving. That is why Jesus' obedience, by destroying in us the roots of sin and restoring to us the freedom to obey the Father totally, gives us back the freedom of the children of God, a freedom which unfolds in praise, adoration and self-offering. [7]

What is it in us that must die so that we might live with more freedom? However we are uniquely and personally being called to die and to rise with Jesus, we realise that this movement renders us vulnerable. The call of Jesus to die and to rise with him takes us to the place where we both hurt and hope at one and the same time. This is the sacred place of encounter – what I refer to, whatever our gender, as the 'womb of our own spirit', the place in which the Word of God is conceived spiritually in each of us.

---

4   Benedict XVI, *Deus caritas est*, 'God is Love" Encyclical Letter, (25 December 2005), n. 6.

5   Paul J. Philibert, *The Priesthood of the Faithful: Key to a living church* (Liturgical Press, 2005), 26.

6   Buambach's phrase is cited by Philibert, *The Priesthood of the Faithful*, 22.

7   Jean-Claude Sagne, 'Christian Obedience and Acceptance of Death,' in *Spirituality: Christian Obedience*, edited by Christian Duquoc and Cassiano Floristan, *Concilium* 139 (New York: Seabury Press 1980), 49.

The Anglican writer, John V Taylor speaks of this context

> The Spirit does not give itself where our encounters are glib, masked exchanges of second-hand thoughts. Our defenses must be down, broken either by intense joy or by despair. One way or the other we must come to the end of ourselves. So this shameful humiliation of Christians, not only in our generation but at all times, is better than self-congratulation, for it is the pre-requisite for a renewal of the Holy Spirit. It is worth remembering that the root of the word humiliation and humility is *humus*. To be down in the straw and the dung and the refuse in Paul's words is to become the soil in which the seed of Christ's manhood falls and dies and brings forth the harvest.[8]

Our dying and rising render us vulnerable and our vulnerability renders us receptive. This overturns our ordinary way of thinking about spiritual growth. It means that we grow spiritually not by starting at the bottom and building something like a spiritual skyscraper. Rather we start at the top and have each floor of our illusory skyscraper pulled out from under us until there is only ourselves in total openness to the Mercy of God.

This leads us to that rather astounding pronouncement of Sebastian Moore when he wrote, 'We need conversion not so much from sin as we need conversion from innocence.'[9] What does he mean by this but that we all need to realise in some way that it is in our failures that life actually begins for us because our failures expose us to our truth: that we are vulnerable, that we are not in control, that we are not self-sufficient, that we are not complete, and that we stand in need of Another, ultimately the very Mercy of God.

Thus, we are called by the Word of God into ministry not as perfect people but as vulnerable people. This is an invitation to move beyond that false expectation that we place on ourselves, but which God never

---

8   John V. Taylor, *The Go-Between God* (London: SCM Press, 1972), 128.

9   Sebastian Moore, *Jesus, the Liberator of Desire* (New York: Crossroad, 1989), 37.

places on us, that we would have 'it all together.' It is the humility eloquently expressed in those oft-quoted words of Oscar Romero:

> It helps now and then to step back and take the long view. The Kingdom is not only beyond our efforts, it is beyond our vision. We accomplish in our lifetime only a tiny fraction of the magnificent enterprise that is God's work. Nothing we do is complete, which is another way of saying that the Kingdom always lies beyond us. No statement says all that could be said. No prayer fully expresses our faith. No confession brings perfection, no pastoral visit brings wholeness. No program accomplishes the Church's mission. No set of goals and objectives includes everything. This is what we are about. We plant the seeds that one day will grow. We water seeds already planted, knowing that they hold future promise. We lay foundations that will need further development. We produce yeast that produces effects far beyond our capabilities. We cannot do everything, and there is a sense of liberation in realizing that. This enables us to do something, and to do it very well. It may be incomplete, but it is a beginning, a step along the way, an opportunity for the Lord's grace to enter and do the rest. We may never see the end results. But that is the difference between the master builder and the worker. We are workers, not master builders, ministers not Messiahs.[10]

There is a part of us that wants to keep accusing ourselves that we are not adequate enough, not effective enough. We find it so very hard to realise that in God there is no accusation. Jesus portrays this beautifully in his encounter with the woman caught in adultery (Jn. 8:3-11). She is flung before Jesus by all her accusers. In response he bends down and doodles in the sand. He refuses to buy into the cycle of accusation. His silence allows the woman to see herself as she is, loved and accepted, and provides her with the space to rise to a new way of living. In this context, Jürgen Moltmann provocatively rephrases Psalm 23:

> So who shall ascend the hill of the Lord? I should like to read the psalm differently [from the version which answers the one

---

10   Oscar Romero, http://www.calprov.org/vocations/vocationsreflections.html, accessed 23 June 2005.

with cleans hands and pure heart]. It is the person who has guilty hands and is grasped by the outstretched hands of Christ who will ascend that hill. Who shall stand in his holy place? I should like to answer that it is the person with an impure heart which has become clear and joyful in the beauty of Christ's grace who can stand the test. Who is the king of glory? He is the Lord, strong in his love and mighty in his self-giving, the Lord, lovely in the way he comes to meet us. His beauty will redeem the world.[11]

It is the beauty of the Lord, the one Word of the Father, the Word of acceptance, of dignity, of love, of desire that gives us that space in which our vulnerability might be transformed into hospitality. When vulnerability is transformed into hospitality there the Kingdom of God most brilliantly shines in the world. Such brings us to the heart of ministry which particularly bears the capacity for vulnerability-become-hospitality. Vulnerability-become-hospitality is the secret of communion, the Communion upon which we gaze in the icon of the Trinity. Here, each is vulnerable in self-giving love to the Other in unrelenting hospitality to one another. Each gives and receives the other.

What then is the outcome for us of a vulnerability-become-a-hospitality? To turn again to Moltmann:

This is no longer the glory of victory, it is the splendour of peace. It is no longer the power of panzas and rockets, it is the force of help. This is no longer the love of power, but the power of love. This is not the riches that make many poor, but the poverty of God which makes many rich. Anyone who hopes for the future of this Lord – poor, and riding upon an ass – does not themselves become strong in performance and achievement or mighty in the competitive struggle. They become receptive in love, open in participation, and vulnerable in community and fellowship.[12]

---

11   Jürgen Moltmann, 'Openness for the Coming God', in *The Power of the Powerless: The word of liberation for today* (San Francisco: Harper and Row, Publishers, 1983), 26.

12   Moltmann, 'Openness for the Coming God', 23.

We enter into our ministry not by conquest but by participation; not by lordship but by fellowship; not by productivity but by receptivity[13] – by a vulnerability-become-a-hospitality forged in our discipleship of the Lord, both Crucified and Risen. Perhaps this brings us to the heart of 'the wounded healer' first described by Henri Nouwen.[14] The wounded healer is the one who can celebrate their common humanity with those to whom they minister – albeit with great sensitivity and pastoral responsibility.[15]

Against this consideration, it is important for us at this point where we feel particularly vulnerable to recognise that healing comes when we give to someone else what we don't have. I recall reading this somewhere for the first time and thinking there must have been a printing error. This presents as a contradiction to what we instinctively think. We easily think we heal from what we have. We give from what we have. This is a fundamental psychological law. However, coming across the insight for a second time unexpectedly, I wonder if it is, in fact, the opposite. Healing comes when giving to someone else what you don't have. There is in this paradox, a gospel truth.

Given all that we have experienced in ministry we might not have a great deal of confidence, we might not have much certainty. We may suffer even from a loss of self-respect. But when we give these experiences to others through the quality of our relationship, by our hospitality, we are surprised. Our vulnerability-become-a-hospitality releases life. Our vulnerable ministry manifests the God who is vulnerable but who is also Promise and Life. We receive life in return for life. Where we see shame, we offer dignity; where we encounter despair, we bring hope; where we find bitterness we suggest forgiveness; in those places of estrangement we offer embrace. The Christian minister searches

---

13 See Jürgen Moltmann, *The Trinity and the Kingdom: The doctrine of God,* translated by Margaret Kohl, (San Francisco: Harper, 1991), 9.

14 See Henri J. M. Nouwen, *The Wounded Healer: Ministry in contemporary society* (New York: Image Books, 1990, originally published by Doubleday, 1972).

15 See Anne Game and Andrew Metcalfe, 'Hospitality: How Woundedness Heals', *Journal of Spirituality and Mental Health* 12 (2010:1), 25-42.

for these places, listens for them, identifies them. In the new order of relationship created by such ministry, the Kingdom comes about. To gaze upon the Trinity is thus to hope for the Kingdom which is the Trinity's realization among us.

As we gaze upon the one Word ever spoken by the Father, Jesus in whom all else is given, and as we take the cup that he offers us to drink, let us pray with St. Clare of Assisi as she urged her sister, Agnes,

> Look upon Him Who became contemptible for you, and follow him . . . Your Spouse, though more beautiful than the children of men became, for your salvation, the lowest of men, despised, struck, scourged untold times throughout His whole body, and then died amid the sufferings of the Cross, O most noble Queen, gaze upon [Him], consider [Him], contemplate [Him] as you desire to imitate [Him].

> If you suffer with Him you shall reign with Him; [if you] weep [with Him], you shall rejoice with Him; [if you] die [with Him] on the cross of tribulation, you shall possess heavenly mansions in the splendor of the saints, and, in the Book of Life, your name shall be called glorious among men.[16]

> Look at the parameters of this mirror, that is, the poverty of Him Who was placed in a manger and wrapped in swaddling clothes. O marvelous humility, O astonishing poverty! The King of the angels, the Lord of heaven and earth, is laid in a manger! Then, at the surface of the mirror, dwell on the holy humility . . . . Then in the depths of this same mirror, contemplate the ineffable charity which led Him to suffer on the wood of the Cross . . . From this moment, then, O queen of our heavenly King, let yourself be inflamed more strongly with the fervor of charity!'[17]

16   Clare of Assisi, 'The Second Letter to Blessed Agnes of Prague', in *Francis and Clare: The complete works*, translated and introduced by Regis J. Armstrong and Ignatius C. Brady, (New York, Ramsey, Toronto: Paulist Press, 1982), 197.

17   Clare of Assisi, 'The Fourth Letter to Blessed Agnes of Prague', in *Francis and Clare*, 204-205.

CHAPTER FOUR

LIVING THE MERCY
OF THE FATHER

*Praised be the God and Father of our Lord Jesus Christ, who has
blessed us in the heavenly realms with every spiritual blessing in
Christ. For he chose us in him before the creation of the world to be
holy and blameless in his sight.*

(*Eph* 1:3-4)

Through Jesus, with him, in him we are brought to the Father. As
Pope John Paul II wrote, 'The whole of the Christian life is like a great
pilgrimage to the house of the Father, whose unconditional love for
every human creature, and in particular for the 'prodigal son' we discover
anew each day. This pilgrimage takes place in the heart of each person,
extends to the believing community and then reaches to the whole of
humanity.'[1] Our gaze on Jesus brings us into his own experience of the
Father, so that Jesus' experience becomes our experience. It is Jesus' own
experience of his Father into which we are growing in and through our
discipleship of Jesus. This is Jesus' gift to us: that in the Spirit we might
enjoy that same experience of the Father that he has. Further, this is the
miracle of the icon of Rublev. The more we gaze upon Jesus in Rublev's
icon we realise that the centre of the icon subtly shifts. At first we think
the centre of the icon is the figure of Jesus in the middle. However, as
we follow his gaze the orientation of the circle pivots, and we begin to
realise that the centre of the circle is actually the figure on the left, the
figure of the Father, the source and origin of all life.

We are brought by Jesus to the Father. Who is the Father? Like the
very word 'God', 'Father' is a complex word because we can project so

1   John John Paul II, *Tertio millennio adveniente* 'Towards the Third Millennium', Apostolic Letter, (10
November, 1994), 49.

much of our own experience of fatherhood onto it. So, when we are talking about the Father of Jesus we have to recognise we are not talking about any father, but the Father of the Son who is Jesus.[2] It is Jesus, and only Jesus, who reveals to us what the divine Father is like. We know the Father only through the Son, and when we gaze upon the Son we begin to see what the Father is like.

> No one knows the Son except the Father, and no one knows the Father except the Son and those to whom the Son chooses to reveal him (*Mt* 11: 27).

If the Son is the Poor One, one with us in our vulnerability and in our suffering, this Father to whom we are brought in the icon is similarly characterised. St Paul expresses this recognition of the type of Fatherhood that exists in God by exclusively linking the Fatherhood of God with the Mercy of God. 'God the Father of mercies' we read constantly in Paul.

> Praise be to the God and Father of our Lord Jesus Christ, the Father of compassion and the God of all comfort (*2 Cor* 1:3).

This is important because, following an argument of Moltmann's, we often say and think – even in our prayer and in our liturgy – 'God, all powerful Father.' But St. Paul never associates the Father of Jesus with power, only with mercy. As Moltmann illustrates, regretfully, the Roman understanding of fatherhood, as the *paterfamilias*, the all powerful lord of the household, the one who had total control and domination over all he possesses, has crept into our Christian understanding and obscured this more original sense of Father being only associated with the quality of mercy – the quality that shines forth in the vulnerability displayed in the Son, Jesus.

This Mercy of the Father is the compassion that Jesus feels within himself; it is the compassion which seeks expression in each of us who is brought by Jesus to the Father of mercies. It is the compassion that

---

2   For the following presentation of 'fatherhood' in God I am indebted to the work of Jürgen Moltmann. See Jürgen Moltmann, *History and the Triune God: Contributions to Trinitarian Theology* (New York: Crossroad, 1992), 4-25.

animates our own lives of ministry. We are to be bearers of the Mercy of the Father. How might we understand the nature of the Mercy that we bear in our ministry? I would suggest that Mercy is born in grief which it transforms into hope. Mercy begins in grief and ends in hope. Therefore, our ministries of Mercy carry within themselves both grief and hope.

If Mercy is the quality of the Father, and if it is that which belongs the very life of God, we can be so bold as to suggest that there is a grief that belongs to God's own very life. This is not the idea of God we get from the Greeks – the idea of a god in whom there is no suffering. It is the Semitic understanding of God, however, that God does not remain unaffected by suffering. The life of God is stirred in the encounter with suffering. This suffering is a certain grief – grief for what has been lost, grief for what could be but which is obstructed by negative forces. As Karen Dresher writes,

> Search the Scriptures,
> for in them you will find
> this God of the loveless,
> this God of Mercy, Love and Justice,
> who weeps over these her children,
> these her precious ones who have been carried from the womb,
> who gathers up her young upon her wings
> and rides along the high places of the earth,
> who sees their suffering
> and cries out like a woman in travail,
> who gasps and pants;
> for with this God,
> any injustice that befalls one of these precious ones
> is never the substance
> of rational reflection and critical analysis,
> but is the source
> of a catastrophic convulsion within the very life of God.[3]

---

3   Karen Dresher, cited in Terence E. Fretheim, *The Suffering of God: An Old Testament perspective* (Philadelphia: Fortress Press, 1984), opening pages.

The Father's life is not unaffected by the encounter with suffering. Such encounter creates a grief within the very life of God. Our own ministry is in response to the grief which is the Father's Mercy. Through us, and in us, the Divine Grief finds its expression in the world, and works to address the experience of suffering that we ourselves encounter.

For us, this participation in the Mercy of the Father, born of grief, is linked with memory. As Metz declares,

> the memory of suffering [is] our critical tool for survival . . . The Christian memory of suffering is dangerous because it warns us where things have gone wrong and challenges our comfort in the official story. The memory of suffering, our own and especially that of others, connects each with the other and provides a practical warning system about distorted relationships, institutions and situations. . . . And this memory impels us to a solidarity with victims.[4]

Thus, with and in the Mercy of the Father, we become awake to the pain of those suffering, the pain of all those who are too inconvenient for those with power and resource to take much notice. In our ministries bearing the Mercy of the Father, grief greets us – if we look – in those parts of our country in which the fog of hopelessness, grief and rage suffocate whole communities. It is there for us to hear in our own neighbourhood where people live lives of quiet desperation through the agony of loneliness, depression or tormenting physical and emotional pain. We hear the grief, too, of the planet struggling to breathe. Then, there is the grief of our Church as we continue to confront the reality of people's pain consequent to their experience of abuse. The heart of Mercy holds this agony. We hold the agony within the hearts of so many and in the pain of our own hearts.

Mercy combines grief and memory to form what Metz calls a 'political spirituality':

---

4   John K. Downey, 'Introduction,' *Love's Strategy: The political theology of Johann Baptist Metz* edited by John K. Downey, (Harrisburg, Pennsylvania: Trinity Press International, 1999), 8.

Christian witnessing to God is guided through and through by political spirituality, a political mysticism. Not a mysticism of political power and political domination, but rather – to speak metaphorically – a mysticism of open or opened eyes. Not only the ears for hearing, but also the eyes are organs of grace! … In the end Jesus did not teach an ascending mysticism of closed eyes but rather a God-mysticism with an increasing readiness for perceiving, a mysticism of open eyes, which sees more and not less.[5]

This mysticism of open eyes awakens us as the heart of Mercy awakens us. But to what are we awakened? Again, to turn to Metz:

It is a mysticism that especially makes visible all invisible and inconvenient suffering, and – convenient or not – pays attention to it and takes responsibility for it, for the sake of a God who is a friend to human beings. . . Such witnessing to God is not allowed political innocence. In the end, witness is intimately involved, with eyes that see, in that history where people are crucified and tortured, hated and miserly loved . . .[6]

We hold the body of the Crucified One when we hold the agony of those who are now crucified by the world's greed, by the world's neglect. We see that dead, abandoned body of Jesus, surrendered into the Father's Mercy, in the world's agony now. We see the body of the crucified One in those whom the world has abandoned, in those parts of our own hearts that are broken.

This ministerial preference for those crucified, and the way in which they are brought to the fore of our ministerial concern, is powerfully expressed in the story of the third century martyrdom of St. Laurence. Laurence, having charge of the Roman community's goods, was summoned by the Roman prefect to give over the treasures that the official believed were in the possession of the community but which

---

5   Johannes Metz, *A Passion for God: The Mystical-Political Dimension of Christianity*, edited and translated by J. Matthew Ashley (Mahwah, New Jersey: Paulist Press, 1999), 163.

6   Metz, *A Passion for God*, 163.

had been distributed to the poor of the city after the martyrdom the previous year. St Laurence replied, without showing any concern, 'The church is rich indeed, nor has any emperor any treasure equal to what it possesses. I will show you a valuable part; but allow me a little time to set everything in order and to make an inventory.' The Prefect did not understand of what treasure Laurence spoke but gave him three days to gather the treasure and to bring it before him. Subsequently Laurence went all over the city, seeking out in every street the decrepit, the blind, the lame, the maimed, the lepers – the poor of every kind – and placed them in rows. He then went to the Prefect and invited him to take possession of the Church's treasures. The Prefect, upon the sight and not amused, demanded of Laurence that he explain and present the treasures that he had ordered Laurence to present him. The original version of Butler's account has St Laurence answering, 'What are you displeased at? *Behold in these poor persons the treasures which I promised to show you . . . the church has no other riches; make use of them for the advantage of Rome, of the emperor and of yourself.'* [Italics mine][7]

What does this ancient story remind us of but that the marginalised, the alienated, those who dwell on the fringe, those who have nothing, who are kept down by the social and political structures, those who are powerless, without voice, defenseless and manipulated by those with power, are the riches of the Christian community because, as Megan McKenna remarks, we believe in a God of Mercy who has manifested his power most fully in those who are poor:

> The ones we don't expect much of , the ones we overlook, the ones we react poorly to, the ones we don't want to be associated with, the ones we despise, the ones we separate ourselves from, the ones we don't want to be with – *them,* whoever they are – are the ones who teach and evangelise us. They are the presence of God in our midst. They are the ones who hold the future in

---

7   For a revised account of the story, see *Butler's Lives of the Saints,* 'August', new full edition, revised by John Cumming (London: Burns & Oates/Collegeville, Minnesota: The Liturgical Press, 1998), 79.

their lacks, in their hearts, and in their nearness to God. They are the poor, the privileged ones of the kingdom, the ones that God pities first and most thoroughly.[Italics in the original][8]

As in Laurence's time, so now, too. The future of the Church lies with those 'outside' because the future of the Kingdom lies with them, drawing them with profound hospitality into the Circle of Love which is our God. To recognise that the Kingdom of God originates from the poor means that we must develop relationship with those on the margins and be evangelised by them. It means listening to them, not for their sakes but for our sakes. It means entering conversation with them in such a way that we risk being changed by them, discovering that the Kingdom of God may already be present within them though they have not been able to name it. We must be constantly goaded in our ministry by the question of who are the modern poor, that is, who are the modern marginalised? Who are those labeled by society and rendered unacceptable? Who are the poor in my own community, in our own society?

More generally, this movement ultimately to justice is a most important place we need to listen for God's coming into our world. The place of the poor is that place we must look towards particularly attentively.

> If we see the Almighty in trinitarian terms, he is not the archetype of the mighty ones of this world. He is the Father of the Christ who was crucified and raised for us. As the Father of Jesus Christ, he is almighty because he exposes himself to the experience of suffering, pain, helplessness and death. But what he is not is almighty power; he is love. It is his passionate, passible love that is almighty … The glory of the triune God is reflected, not in the crowns of kings and triumphs of victors, but in the face of the crucified Jesus, and in the faces of the oppressed whose brother he became. He is the one visible image of the invisible God. The

---

8   Megan McKenna, *Not Counting Women and Children* (Maryknoll, New York: Orbis, 1994), 19.

glory of the triune God is also reflected in the community of Christ: in the fellowship of believers and of the poor.[9]

As we hold the agony of others and as we hold our own agony, we are full of question. With the heart of the Father's Mercy we gaze towards heaven. And no answer comes. Yet now, as on that first Good Friday in the surrender of the Son to the Father, the Silence calls forth a depth of hope we barely imagined possible and our hope fills the Silence. It is our hope that fills the Silence. The heart of Mercy holds the world's agony but it also allows hope to rise. It cannot avoid the question that it might be a hope in vain. In the face of what agony we encounter and that we bear, our hope is not given an easy, facile answer or consolation. We must wait in our hope. Nonetheless, in our waiting, full of surrender into the Father of Mercies, our hope begins to transform our grief. Mercy transforms grief into hope. Mercy is, therefore, thoroughly paschal in character. It looks squarely at death and affirms life. It looks at absence and proclaims presence. It stands at dead ends and celebrates new beginnings. Mercy is the midwife delivering hope from the body of grief.

As Mercy acts as midwife in this way, we recognise its feminine characteristic. Mercy is the same word in Hebrew as womb. Thus, as Moltmann points out when we come to think of God as Father we really need to have the sense of the 'motherly fatherliness' of God.'[10] Only a term like this in some way adequately describes the kind of Father we are talking about when we address the Christian God as 'Father.'

How might we understand more fully the nature of the Father's motherliness? There is a wonderful scene in Sean Penn's powerful and brilliant film, 'Dead Man Walking.' The story is a film about a religious sister's journey with a prisoner on death row in the days leading up to his execution. Helen Prejean is involved simply in response to his request for help. It is all new for her and she feels well out of her depth.

9   Jürgen Moltmann, *The Trinity and the Kingdom*, (San Francisco: Harper and Row, 1981), 197-198.

10   See Moltmann, *History and the Triune God*, 19-25.

There is a scene which represents her struggle. She is at the family home resting in a fitful sleep and her own mother comes to see how she is. As Helen discusses with her mother all that is happening and how difficult it is to get close to Matt Poncelet, the prisoner, her mother recounts the story of many years earlier how Helen gave her a black eye. Helen had been in a fever and delirious. Her mother recounts her response to the whack that she had been given. 'I held you tight, and the more you fought the tighter I held you. I would not let you go.' It was a wonderful statement about the relationship of love between mother and daughter, just as it was an analogy about what Helen was being called to do with the prisoner. It is also a wonderful statement about God's relationship with us: the God who holds us tight, who will not let us go even though we are struggling, lashing out and to all intent and purpose, giving him 'black eyes'! This is the motherly fatherliness of our God, revealed by the Vulnerable One who is Jesus.

In the embrace of the Father we are fully accepted. The Father is not afraid of our evil in the same way that we are. Through his Son, Jesus, the Father has been to the places of evil. Ultimately, he has visited that place of total God-forsakeness which is Calvary and manifested his glory precisely there. There are many other occasions in the gospels, though, where God, in Jesus, has gone to the places of darkness: the desert, the land of the dead where the Geresene demoniac lives and howls, the tomb where Lazarus lies. God the Father is not afraid of our darkness, the ways in which our sinfulness expresses itself. God, the 'motherly Father', holds us even though we hit out at the embrace. This is because God the 'motherly Father' always sees the whole picture. He sees beyond our action. He understands the complex forces that constitute so much of our action, and he keeps seeing what he has made: person, unique and eternal – a person who has a goodness and a beauty and a sacredness beyond even his worst acts.

To be brought to the Father of mercies is to live with both grief and hope. A ministry reflecting the Mercy of the Father is the one, therefore, which has listened ever so deeply, reverently and attentively to the true situation of people and spoken out a word in which the people can recognise their deepest truth and humanity. The voice of such Mercy invites; it opens up new vistas, new horizons for the imagination. To borrow for this context Mercy resists all those forces in ourselves and around us that work to squash life, to destroy life, or to borrow the words of the Australian theologian, Tony Kelly for this context, Mercy, 'means to be a constant protest against anything that would truncate our humanity, mutilate our sensitivities or stunt the creativity of the imagination.'[11]

Mercy, however, is thoroughly practical in character. I think of the Australian journalist Cathy Matthews' account of how the survivors of a horrific and tragic bushfire in the state of Victoria continued to pick up the pieces or their lives, enabling each other with new beginnings in the face of their own experience of grief:

> School principals work hard to keep children learning and to give them a sense of security. The demountable buildings hastily erected are hard to heat, yet children show their resilience and their innocence. It is rewarding to witness. They search their mothers' faces at day's end to be sure everything is OK.

> When mothers cannot find the strength to cook a meal, they go to the Kinglake central diner where some wonderful person is providing a roast meal every night for $15 a family. The meal nurtures the children and companionship nourishes the parents for an hour or two to shorten the cold night ahead.

> There have been fine acts of kindness. The Baptist minister runs from one end of his day to the next, caring for grieving children one minute and helping rebuild fences the next.

> . . . I urge one of his young congregation to start a youth program in Kinglake's one surviving building so the youth have an activity one night a week, at least. . . She has taken it a step further,

---

11   Anthony Kelly, *A New Imagining: Towards an Australian spirituality* (Melbourne: Collins Dove, 1990), 18.

enrolling in a youth leadership course. She knows she will get far more out of it than she puts in.

Her mother plans a weekly cooking bee to get soups and hearty stews up the mountain each Sunday to those caravans in lonely clearings, cheering those who while away their evenings alone. The peppermint gums are beginning to shoot, and the bright green leaves of ferns are showing through. A sign of life's resilience, of the cycles nature promises. And of hope. [12]

The Mercy of the Father is thus demonstrated in very concrete ways. We illustrate it whenever we replace domination with service, competition with mutuality, cold efficiency with attentiveness, profit-led productivity with compassion. It happens whenever we refuse to let cynicism squash our hope; fear overwhelm our love; bitterness overrule our openness, vengeance overtake our forgiveness; convenience and security replace truthfulness. When we make decisions for hope, for love, for openness, for forgiveness and truth we are affirming life. We are turning the place of grief into hope, death into a place of life. And we are experiencing the power of the Resurrection in our own life.

Living with the Mercy of the Father also means, practically, to live with forgiveness. Forgiveness perhaps expresses most powerfully what it means to live with the Mercy of the Father. Forgiveness is at the heart of the gospel; it is central to the preaching and ministry of Jesus. Why? It is at the centre, perhaps, because it is the strategy par excellence of Communion. We cannot experience communion with one another without travelling the difficult road of forgiveness. The journey into the Communion which is God's own very life as Trinity is one that will constantly ask us to enter into the mystery of forgiveness.

I raise this consideration here because a ministry which bears the Mercy of the Father will often have to confront the struggle in the lives of others around forgiveness. However, we have to be very clear what

---

12   Cathy Matthews, 'Matchstick Memories', *The Sydney Morning Herald*, Weekend Edition (May 23-24, 2009), News Review 5.

forgiveness is, and what it is not. Firstly, forgiveness is not a feeling. We may never feel forgiving; we do not need to feel forgiving in order to forgive. There are some hurts that we will experience in our life which will always generate painful feelings and we do not have to get over these feelings before we forgive. Neither does forgiveness mean that we forget our hurts. Again, some hurts are altogether too deep, too painful, to forget. There are some hurts we should never forget. What makes the difference is not whether we have memories of being hurt or not but how we deal with our memories of being hurt.

So what is forgiveness from a Christian perspective? It is the decision and the action to remain open to the one who has hurt me, not to exclude them, not to isolate them, not to cast them out of the possibility of living into the experience of communion once again. As Miroslav Volf identities, the key to Christian forgiveness is a certain repentance.[13] 'Repent and believe the Good News,' (Mk 1:15) is what Jesus proclaims at the outset of his ministry. Curiously, Jesus preaches repentance in Galilee, the land of the oppressed. The reaction of those who first heard the message must have been along the lines, 'What have we to repent of? We are the oppressed. We have nothing to repent! Go preach the message to those who are oppressing us. They are the ones who are doing us wrong. They are the ones who have something to repent!' As Volf points out, however, it is not to the oppressor that Jesus preaches repentance; it is to the oppressed. What have they to repent? They are to repent of the instinct for revenge. For revenge begets revenge, and the circle of violence, of domination and submission, of exclusion and isolation is perpetuated.

Jesus invites the Galileans in the face of their hurt to let go of their instinct for vengeance. He invites us to do the same. This is the first step of the journey of forgiveness: to let go of the instinct to strike up, to hit back, to have revenge.

---

13   See Miroslav Volf, *Exclusion and Embrace: A Theological Exploration of Identity, Otherness, and Reconciliation.* (Nashville: Abingdon Press, 1996), 111-125.

When we let go of the tendency for revenge then we create a space in which there exists at least the possibility for justice. In this space there is the possibility for the cycle of violence and exclusion to cease, for the one who has hurt me to recognise their actions and to redress the situation. The possibility of true justice can only occur when we have stopped the cycle of vengeance. We saw this extraordinarily demonstrated in South Africa. I think of one of the stories before the Truth and Reconciliation Commission.[14]

> There was a black woman who had to testify in the way that she had been brutally mistreated by a group of white security officers, one of whom, Mr. Van de Broek, had just been tried and found implicated in the murders of both the woman's son and husband some years before.
>
> It was indeed Mr. Van de Broek, it had been established, who had come to the woman's home many years back, had taken her son, shot him at point blank range and then burned the young man's body on a fire while he and his officers partied. Seven years later, Van de Broek and his cohorts had returned to take away her husband as well. For many months she heard nothing of his whereabouts. Then almost two years after her husband's disappearance, Van de Broek came back to fetch the woman herself. How vividly she remembers that evening, going to a place beside the river, where she was shown her husband, bound and beaten but still strong in spirit, lying on a pile of wood. The last words she heard from his lips, as the officer poured gasoline over his body and set him aflame, were, 'Father, forgive them.'
>
> And now the woman stands in the courtroom and listens to the confession offered by Mr. Van de Broek. A member of the commission turns to her and asks, 'So, what do you want? How can justice be done to this man who has so brutally destroyed your family?'

---

14   Taken from John McSweeney, *Call Me David: Bishop David Cremin, a memoir* (Kingsgrove, NSW: OMP Publications, 2008), 137-139.

'I want three things,' begins the old woman, calmly but confidently. 'I want first to be taken to the place where my husband's body was burned so that I can gather the dust and give his remains a decent burial.' She pauses, then continues, 'My husband and son were my only family. I want secondly, therefore, for Mr. Van de Broek to become my son. I would like him to come twice a month to the ghetto and spend a time with me so that I can pour out on him whatever love I have remaining with me.

'And finally,' she says, 'I want a third thing. I would like Mr. Van de Broek to know that I offer him forgiveness because Jesus Christ died to forgive. This was also the wish of my husband. And so, I would kindly ask someone to come to my side and lead me across the courtroom so that I can take Mr. Van de Broek in my arms, embrace him and let him know he is truly forgiven.'

In another example we also see the power of such forgiveness. In 1995 seven Trappist monks were murdered by Islamic extremists in Algeria. Twelve months earlier, the abbot of the community, Dom Christian, had written a poem of forgiveness. It was his last will and testament to be opened in Paris should the worse come to worst. He called it, 'When we face an A-DIEU.'

If it should happen one day – and it could be today –
that I become a victim of the terrorism which now seems ready to engulf
all the foreigners living in Algeria,
I would like my community, my Church and my family
to remember that my life was GIVEN to God and to this country.
I ask them to accept the fact that the One Master of all life
was not a stranger to this brutal departure.
I would ask them to pray for me:
for how could I be found worthy of such an offering?
I ask them to associate this death with so many other equally violent ones
which are forgotten through indifference or anonymity . . .

> . . . And also you, my last-minute friend, who will not have known
> what you were doing:
> Yes, I want this THANK YOU and this 'A-DIEU to be for you, too,
> because in God's face I see yours.
> May we meet again as happy thieves in Paradise, if it please God,
> the Father of us both. [15]

'Christian' in name and Christian in deed, this monk gives extraordinary witness to the power of forgiveness. The one who had spent his life in attentiveness meets the Divine Lion at the moment of his death through his grace given capacity to forgive.

In stories such as these we taste the full power of Christian forgiveness. We may not find ourselves in such dramatic circumstances but every day living in community brings with it the challenge of forgiveness. Life in Christian community is the primary way in which God prepares us to participate in the mystery of triune love. Christian community 'is the fiery forge in which God tempers our personalities and gets them ready to share more deeply in the fullness of divine community . . . To use an example from the Catholic mystical tradition it *purges* us of our imperfections, *illumines* us along our journey through life, and eventually brings us to state of *union* with God.'[16]

It is also in the day-to-day grind of forgiveness that we realise that community life is not something we create but something that we receive as gift from God. We realise, to use Bonhoeffer's words, that it is not an ideal for which we strive, but a divine reality we experience. He writes,

> By sheer grace God will not permit us to live even for a brief period
> in a dream world. He does not abandon us to those rapturous
> experiences and lofty moods that come over us like a dream.
> God is not a God of the emotions but a God of truth. Only that

---

15 'Testament of Father Christian', in Bernardo Oivera, *How to Follow: The martyrs of Atlas* (Petersham, Massachusetts: St. Bede's Publications, 1997), 127, 129. The story of the monks is wonderfully recounted in the French film by Xavier Beauvois, *Of Gods and Men*, (Sony Pictures Classics, 2010).

16 Dennis J. Billy, 'Called to Community', *Review for Religious* 54 (May-June 1995), 374.

fellowship that faces such disillusionment, with all its unhappy and ugly aspects, begins to be what it should be in God's sight, begins to grasp in faith the promise that is given to it. . . .

. . . Thus the very hour of disillusionment with my brother becomes incomparably salutary, because it so thoroughly teaches me that neither of us can ever live by our own words and deeds, but only by that one Word and Deed which really binds us together – the forgiveness of sins in Jesus Christ. When the morning mists of dreams vanish, then dawns the bright day of Christian fellowship.[17]

May that day dawn for each of us in our constant readiness to forgive one another, in the recognition that in the death of fear love rises, in the death of shame rises dignity, in the death of resentment rises fellowship.

We should not be surprised that forgiveness is the final act of Jesus on the Cross before his surrender to the Father. It is his deepest affirmation of life, his final act of resistance to all those forces that would create alienation, estrangement, separation, isolation. Against all those forces, Jesus acts even in the face of death, to create the possibility of communion. Forgiveness is one of the most difficult aspects of our Christian life that we learn but the most important, for in the exercise of forgiveness we show forth in an altogether too real a way whether we actually do believe that God is Communion, and whether we actually do believe that Communion is both our origin and our destiny. As for Jesus, may our own readiness to forgive be our act of resistance to all that would inhibit the possibility of the Communion of which our ministry is at service.

Thus, may our ministries truly bear the Mercy of the Father.

CHAPTER FIVE

THE SPIRIT OF NEW FRONTIERS

Again Jesus said, 'Peace be with you! As the Father has sent me, I am sending you.' And with that he breathed on them and said, 'Receive the Holy Spirit. If you forgive anyone's sins, their sins are forgiven; if you do not forgive them, they are not forgiven.

(*Jn* 20: 21-23)

'The wind blows wherever it pleases,' says Jesus. 'You hear its sound, but you cannot tell where it comes from or where it is going. So it is with everyone born of the Spirit' (*Jn* 3:8). Indeed, the Spirit is transparent like the wind or like a breath. There are the two images of the Spirit, in fact, with which we are presented at the Festival of Pentecost: a forceful wind which shook the house, fire to enflame cold hearts and enable the disciples with courage and confidence. Yet, in the Gospel of the day the Spirit comes in the form of the gentleness of Jesus' breath. This is a wonderful paradox: the Spirit as both a mighty wind and a gentle breath; the Spirit as both this enabling courage and this quiet reassurance which is peace. In each case, the Spirit awakens: either it jolts as a storm, or it acts like the zephyr of air at a moment just before dawn which ever so lightly nuzzles creation into daily life. In either case, we cannot see it but we do we know it by its effects, by what has been stirred, by the way in which we have become more awakened to life, in life, and for life.

In most ways it has been unfortunate that we have termed this Person within the Divine Community of the Trinity as 'spirit.' As Moltmann indicates, whether we talk Greek, Latin, German or English, 'spirit' ordinarily denotes for us something immaterial, disembodied, supersensory. [1] And yet the Divine Spirit is something quite earthy. Its Semitic counterpart, *ruach*, always means something living compared

---

1   See Jürgen Moltmann, *The Spirit of Life: A universal affirmation*, (Minneapolis: Fortress Press, 1992), 40.

with something dead, something moving over against that which is rigid and petrified. 'When you take away their *ruach* they die. When you send forth your *ruach* they are created; and you renew the face of the earth' (Ps 104:29). In the Hebrew mind, *ruach* and *dabar* – God's word – are very close to one another. *Ruach* is thought of as the breath of God's voice. All things are called to life through God's Spirit and Word. And so we read, 'By the word of the Lord the heavens were made, and all their host by the breath of his mouth' (Ps 33: 6). How interesting it is that *dabar* is masculine and *ruach* is feminine: both exist in complementarity.[2]

If the breath of God's voice is the creative power from which everything that has life lives, we can talk, according to Moltmann, of the Spirit as the 'drive' and 'instinct' for life, awakened by God. This is why the Spirit and sexuality are so closely interconnected. The impulse of life, *eros*, is the divine spark within us which calls us into greater participation in creation, with each other and into the wonder of something elsewhere and otherwise than ourselves. By *eros* is meant the force which holds the world together and keeps it alive. It is the most personal expression of the Spirit's life within us.

The Spirit is experienced in us, then, whenever we say 'yes' to life. Moltmann teaches that,

> true spirituality will thus be the restoration of the love for life – that is to say, *vitality*. The full and unreserved 'yes' to life, and the full and unreserved love for the living are the first experiences of God's Spirit. … The spirituality of life breaks through [the] inward numbness [to life], the armour of our indifference, the barriers of our insensitivity to pain. It again breaks open the 'well of life' in us and among us, so that we can weep again and laugh again and love again.[3]

---

2   See Moltmann, *The Spirit of Life*, 42.

3   Moltmann, *The Spirit of Life*, 97.

Paraphrasing and adapting Augustine, Moltmann thus prays:

> When I love God, I love the beauty of bodies, the rhythm of
> movements, the shining of eyes, the embraces, the feelings, the
> scents, the sounds of all this protean creation. When I love you,
> my God, I want to embrace it all, for I love you with all my senses
> in the creations of your love. In all the things that encounter me,
> you are waiting for me. For a long time I looked for you within
> myself, and crept into the shell of my own soul, protecting myself
> with an armour of inapproachability. But you were outside –
> outside myself – and enticed me out of the narrowness of my
> heart into the broad place of love for life. So I came out of myself
> and found my soul in my senses, and my own self in others[4]

Moltmann concludes, 'The more I love God the more gladly I exist.
The more immediately and wholly I exist, the more I sense the living
God, the inexhaustible well of life, and life's eternity.'[5] The end result is
a greater sense of consciousness, of awareness, of aliveness.

It is important to remember though that the Spirit is both celebration
of what has been received as well as the hope of that which we still
await. For in bringing us to greater consciousness the Spirit manifests
that which we had thought impossible. It is the Spirit which animates
the recognition that things can be different, who informs our dreams
and sets ablaze our hope.

In this way the Spirit leads us into ever new horizons. Moltmann
highlights that the word *ruach* is probably related also to another word
rewah, which means breadth.[6] Similarly in English, the *breath* of God's
voice creates *breadth*. It sets in motion. It leads out of narrow places into
wide vistas, and ever greater awareness of life. To experience the Spirit
is to experience then what is divine as space – the space of freedom in
which the person, alive and awake, can move. 'You have set my feet in
a broad place' (*Ps* 31:8). According to Moltmann, in 'Kabbalistic Jewish

4   Moltmann, *The Spirit of Life*, 98.

5   Moltmann, *The Spirit of Life*, 98.

6   See Moltmann, *The Spirit of Life*, 43.

tradition one of God's secret names is MAKOM, the wide space.[7] God is this wide open space in which new and hitherto unsuspected expectations about life are awakened. So the experience of the Spirit is the experience of life's new beginning. St. Ireaneus wrote somewhere that the Christian life is a beginning moving through beginnings to a beginning. This is the source of Christian possibility and the way that we can enter into Kierkegaard's marvelous aspiration – even if tragically he could not personally realise it: 'If I were to wish for something, I would wish not for wealth or power but for the passion of possibility, for the eye, eternally young, eternally ardent, that sees possibility everywhere. Pleasure disappoints; possibility does not.'[8]

As the One who awakens us, who stirs us into life, who sets us in motion into the broad places, and who sustains in a life of beginnings, it is the gift of the Spirit to endow us with new possibilities for mission and creativity in evangelization. Thus the Spirit, the Possibility which is God, commissions us to a renewed sense of the vitality of the Kingdom, a new sense of mission, and a new sense of our ministry.

The Spirit, though, is not simply the One who endows us with an imagination of the possible. We also recognise that the Spirit is the One who also retrieves to us our memory. Indeed, in the Gospel Jesus offers us the Spirit precisely so that we might 'remember'.

> All this I have spoken while still with you. But the Advocate, the Holy Spirit, whom the Father will send in my name, will teach you all things and will remind you of everything I have said to you (*Jn* 14: 25-26).

Subsequently, if we are to respond to the Spirit's invitation to begin anew, to be open to new beginnings, fresh with possibility, we must firstly retrieve our memory. We must listen to our stories again. We must recount all the stories of our communities in which we minister.

---

7   Moltmann, *The Spirit of Life*, 43.

8   Søren Kierkegaard, 'Either/Or, A Fragment of Life', in *The Essential Kierkegaard*, edited by Howard V. Hong and Edna H. Hong (Princeton, New Jersey: Princeton University Press, 2000), 45.

And in the telling of the stories again we might glimpse where we have come from. Without too much analysis we might realise in ourselves that the Spirit has been with us all this time, always pushing us to new possibilities, new beginnings. Yes, something *has* been unfolding within our collective experiences, even at times despite ourselves. This is why the older members of our communities are so precious and are such a gift in our midst. We need to seek creative ways of 'lighting campfires', sitting around together and remembering. This is not just sentimental nostalgia. It is an education in the imagination especially of the newcomers to ministry who learn as they listen and as they laugh at characters they never knew realise they are sharing in a drama much larger that their own selves and ambitions. Who are the storytellers, the guardians of memories, in our community? Let us honour them, for their memories contain the vitality of the future.

We live in a time of transition from one epoch to another which demands an attitude of great dialogue, a dialogue which engages in genuine listening, genuine conversation. This is a dangerous time but it is also a time which we can work with to the Kingdom's advantage. Perhaps at no other time in history has there been such a period when we have the freedom and capacity to imagine newness, new forms, fresh articulations. We enter this dialogue as leaders of our people, faithful to memory and open to fresh vision. The Spirit calls us to be those who remember, fully remember, who savour the memory of Christ Jesus, the memory of the rich tradition which is ours, the lived experience of 2000 years of experience of this person Jesus of Nazareth, the memory of this Triune Mystery which he disclosed. And at the same time the Spirit calls us to be those of vision. In the words of the Irish theologian, Anne Kelly, 'we are a people born of memory and dreaming hope. The tradition within which we find ourselves as theologians comes as the bearer both of memory and possibility. As theologians we share the task of sharing our story and vision with the next generation so that hope and history may rhyme.'[9]

---

9   Anne Kelly, 'The Agenda for Theology in Ireland Today II', *The Furrow* 42 (1991), 699.

This interrelationship between memory and vision, forged by the Spirit, is well demonstrated by an ancient Sufi story.

> Once upon a time – among an ancient people – an only child of a family of thread makers was orphaned. Wandering nomad weavers took the boy into their tribe for a while but, for lack of means, eventually had to sell him as an apprentice to a family of shipbuilders. In their situation, the shipbuilders trained him to make masts. Mastmaking was a good trade, in very great demand in this sailing town.
>
> The young man liked the work, but years later, while on a business voyage for the mastmakers, this same young man – once an orphaned spinner, once an abandoned weaver and now a satisfied mastmaker – was shipwrecked on a primitive island.
>
> And in this place the people lived in wait for the fulfilment of a promise that God would someday send a foreigner who would help them save their religious treasures from ruin by the hostile environment. All other foreigners were to be rejected.
>
> 'Are you the one for whom we wait? Are you the one who will save our religious treasure?' they asked.
>
> At this very moment the young man understood both his past and his future. He took the memory of his experience as a spinner of thread and made rope; he took the memory of his experience as a weaver and made cloth; he took the memory of his experience as a mastmaker and made long, strong poles. And out of all these memories, he fashioned the vision of a tent which saved the values of that people.[10]

As Christian ministers, bearers of the Spirit of possibility, we remember Jesus' journey from death into life, and in that memory, out of that memory, we seek new possibilities for ourselves and for our societies. Marked with memory and vision we are called to be people of possibility, offering to others the possibility that is God.

---

10   Taken from Joan Chittister, *The Winds of Change: Women challenge the Church* (Kansas City, Missouri: Sheed and Ward, 1986), 35-36.

It is the work of the Spirit to lead us forward into new possibilities as we keep 'memory' and 'vision' hand in hand. Part of this collective re-imagining is listening to and respecting that way in which the Spirit has been given to us, the gift that each generation of ministers brings to our communities at this time. Each generation has its own particular memory and imagination. What gift is woven from its experience? Can the rest of us receive that gift and enable it to be realised? We need to construct forums by which we can really share in this kind of exercise, hear and respect each other.

We believe that the Spirit in every generation endows the *communio* with the gifts it requires. What are the gifts in our own group? Cannot only each generation name its gift, communicate that gift and have that gift fully welcomed and enjoyed by all the others, but can we also go around our community and name the gift each individual brings to ministry and the *communio*? People blossom and enjoy vitality when their own unique gift is acknowledged, engaged and encouraged. When we really work at loving each other in this way then we may be surprised at what happens to whatever low morale we may experience. Yes, we may even find our spirits dancing, full of purpose and meaning.

When we offer the word of life to each other we are in a position to offer a word of life to our world. The word we offer then is the word of invitation. It is not a moralising word or a word which condemns but a 'poetic' word, – a word which seizes people's imagination because it deeply respects them and evokes in them the desire for something more, something different, that 'new beginning' which is the mark of the Spirit. This is the word which nurtures, which nourishes and always invites.

> . . . the wisdom that comes from heaven is first of all pure; then peace-loving, considerate, submissive, full of mercy and good fruit, impartial and sincere. Peacemakers who sow in peace reap a harvest of righteousness (*Jas* 3: 17-18).

This is prophetic wisdom. Each of us as a minister is commissioned to speak wih this wisdom – a word offered, as Brueggemann implores, 'neither in rage or cheap grace, but with the candour born of anguish and passion.'[11] We need not fear. If we are speaking such a word people will respond. It is bread for the hungry and the hungry do not ignore quality bread. But if we speak in cliché, giving answers to questions no one is asking, then, to use a famous phrase of Karl Rahner's, our words will fall 'like birds frozen to death and falling from winter skies.'[12] They oppress; they alienate; they petrify. They do not make the lame dance, they do not bring the dead to life, the blind to see and the deaf to hear.

Out of our memory and vision, we are to offer, instead, a 'poetic' word – that word which seizes others' imagination and which can only come through intense listening and waiting. Such watchfulness is imbued with that an analogical imagination, the ability to see similarity in difference. With this imagination, the prophetic minister who speaks out the 'poetic' word listens to people's stories, reads the newspapers, watches the television, listening for the deeper currents, listening for how the presenting story represents the vaster, eternal story of slavery seeking freedom, of death giving way to life, of despair being transformed into possibility and confidence. The analogical imagination is constantly alert to the revelation of God in and through nature, in and through people's ordinary experience. When we approach life with this analogical imagination then we recognise that the stories of Scripture are actually being lived out in front of us, before our own eyes. They are not simply the stories of 2000 years ago. They are the expressions of what the Spirit effects even no in our midst.

This is the imagination at the very base of our understanding of Sacrament. In common water we celebrate new life, a simple meal of bread and wine becomes the presence of the God of love, ordinary oil becomes the presence of divine healing, touch confirms authority, the love of man and woman reflects and makes present the divine Unity. As

---

11   Walter Brueggemann, *The Prophetic Imagination* (Philadelphia: Fortress Press, 1978), 50.

12   Karl Rahner, 'Thoughts on the Theology of Christmas' in Theology of the Spiritual Life, *Theological Investigations* Volume 3. (Baltimore: Helican Press/ London: Darton, Longman and Todd. 1967), 28.

with word, so, too, with our sacramental ritual. When it is celebrated in such a way as to become transparent of its Mystery then once again we will discover people there. Even hungry people, however, will not eat stale bread.

As we stumble and stutter to offer the word of life to both ourselves and to our world, we regain the prophetic voice which belongs to ministry. May we then speak with that same imagination as 'the young Galilean poet of the haunted spirit. He who was able to image the incarnation and inhabit it, and who thereby opened out one of the most amazing imaginative symbols and sources of all time: the Trinity as source of distance and intimacy, belonging and dislocation, selfhood and otherness.'[13]

In our ministry, do we dare to be that passionate?

---

13   John O'Donohue, 'The Agenda for Theology in Ireland Today I', *The Furrow* 42 (1991), 698.

CONCLUSION

GRIEVING AND DANCING

For Jesus himself the invitation to reflect on his ministry came at both welcome and unwelcome times. They are presented to us as both times for Jesus of unwelcome trial and intensity such as when he was driven by the Spirit into the desert (*Mk* 1:12) and as times of apparent familiarity such as we hear of in Luke, when Jesus would make his way to a lonely spot when day broke or when he would spend the night in the hills praying (*Lk* 4:42; 6:12). At other rimes, such as on the occasion of John's arrest (*Mt* 4:12), and then later at John's death, reflective times become ones of surprising re-orientation for Jesus – times of vocational discernment in which the echoes of the Father's will grow in their clarity and direction.

> When Jesus heard what had happened, he withdrew by boat privately to a solitary place. Hearing of this the crowds followed him on foot from the towns. When Jesus landed and saw a large crowd, he had compassion on them and healed their sick (*Mt* 14:13-14).

This chapter in Matthew begins with the death of John the Baptist, an event which acts to clarify Jesus' independence from the mentor from whom Jesus had first sketched the contours of the Kingdom he preached. John's death firmly sets Jesus on his own, just as it indicates to him the price one must pay for assuming a prophetic stance. We can only imagine the turbulence of Jesus' emotion at this time: a volatile mixture of sadness and fear, of loneliness and yet, paradoxically, of purpose. He wants to be alone. Events threaten to overwhelm him. Yet, this retreat becomes for him, in the midst of his own confusion, a moment of clarification. His own concerns are pitched against the hunger of the crowd. His own anxiety is pitched against a much larger backdrop: the urgency of the Kingdom. Here is a real moment of choice for Jesus. He has sought solitude but instead is discovered by the needs of the people. Does he get back into the boat and assume his solitariness or does he stand and face the crowd? Matthew gives us the answer: his heart went out to them. The Greek expresses it with much more eloquence: his bowels churned with pity – this strange combination of compassion and rage by which the Mercy of the Father courses through him. Jesus' choice to stand and face the people's hunger at this occasion is a pivotal moment for him in his life's journey. Here, Jesus' fundamental option is to be a person at the service of the Father's Kingdom over and above his own security. It will be ratified when he sets his gaze irrevocably on Jerusalem (Lk. 9:51) and given its fullest expression in Gethsemane.

I focus on this moment in Jesus' life, because like him, we too are at a tumultuous time in our journey as Christian ministers. Like Jesus we are presented with a choice of spirit which will consolidate or undermine our choice to be ministers of the gospel. Ministerial roles are changing. Structures are changing as they meet a rapidly decreasing clergy number and an emergent lay leadership. In the face of such concern the temptation is to want to get into our own little boat, to once again feel secure and to be consoled, to tame the demands of the Kingdom in ways which retrieve our sense of control, emotionally and spiritually. The example of Jesus, however, calls us beyond where we instinctively prefer to rest, for the Christian never has the luxury of settling, of saying, 'this is enough.'

These times of both excitement and uncertainty lead us to personally and collaboratively ask the hard questions about our ministry. What does it mean to be a minister of the gospel today? How can we minister most effectively to our people? Can our Christian faith survive in this millennium? Many would see no place for Christian faith in this new world. Can the Church continue to be an effective sacrament of the saving mystery of Jesus' death and resurrection? Many are saying no, and are looking for alternative means of spiritual nourishment and meaning and different contexts to engage the questions of their hearts. Can we be in the new millennium at all with a sense of freedom and energy and fresh possibility? Or are we doomed to be enchained to the unresolved tensions of the last two, desperately treading water as we struggle to reach the shores of a certain restorationism? Will the Church, and indeed ministry, breathe in the air of this new millennium and have its lungs expanded?

Each place, no doubt, has its own variations of these questions, given the differing contexts and issues. But the millennium raises them nonetheless. It is an age rightly of crisis: a time to reconsider; a time to be attentive to the tensions; a time to inquire into them; a time to be open to new insights; a time to make new choices and develop new strategies. It is a time of growth.

As Christians, we are never exempt from the presence, at least, of the fear and hope which coexist in tension within our psyches and which rise in our hearts and minds and spirits at any moment of transition in history.

As Christians, though, we are called to go beyond fear. The region beyond fear, though, is not abandonment. Neither is it a defensive fundamentalism. Further, simple stoic endurance is death for us, and for our people; self-pitying lamentation is an indulgence and luxury which is not allowed in the Kingdom. Beyond fear, there is grief. Beyond fear, there is conscious awareness that knows what has passed and what must be let go.

Equally, as Christians we are called to do more than simply hope in the sense of being filled with optimism. Beyond hope, there is celebration, there is dance. Beyond hope there is joyful recognition of what is taking place here, now.

Our faith transforms the instinctive fear and hope we experience at this time into grief and dance. In the light of faith, we are being called to both grieve and to dance. We are being called, I believe, to see 'grief' and 'dance' as the two poles of the tension that is part of every crisis.

As we hear the call to journey into the future once again, we do grieve over the loss of so much by which we have hitherto defined ourselves in ministry. As Gerald Arbuckle asserts, it is a time in which the Western Church is in massive grief and we must be honest about this. We need to acknowledge this, for Arbuckle, quoting Ovid, reminds us that suppressed grief suffocates creativity or openness to newness.[1] Unless grief is owned and acknowledged, particularly in rituals, groups and individuals remain trapped in the past, unable to open themselves to new ways of thinking and acting. Only the person who knows how to grieve, how to enter the experience of deep vulnerability, can receive that promise of resurrection life – the promise being made to us, in this time and in this place.

We can feel bereft. But then, as Cardinal Martini, formerly of Milan, once remarked, the greatest obstacle to faith in the Church today is the ethic of success and of achievement, the ethic which counts numbers and stockpiles of real estate. The American Benedictine, Joan Chittister put it this way to Religious, but I think her sentiment is apt for all ministers as well:

> When religious life we thought looked most alive – when the religious [factory] had reached the peak of the individual model that spawned it, producing products at a great rate and organising thousands – it was actually most dead. And we did not know it. … Schooled in a spirituality … of success we have lost sight of the spirituality of risk; … the courage to go on bereft of those things by which we had become accepted: nice, acceptable positions in clearly defined ministries under comfortable and socially approved conditions. It requires that we give up the idea of coasting into retirement on steadily decreasing responsibilities … it means we go on without success, with no memorials raised to our efforts, with no institutions to mark our accomplishments, with no respect for age, with no certainty that any one at any time will come behind us to complete the task.[2]

---

1   Gerald Arbuckle, 'The Call to Today's Church to Grieve in Hope', *Australasian Catholic Record* 73 (1996:4), 387-393.

2   Joan Chittister, *The Fire in these Ashes* (Kansas City: Sheed and Ward, 1995), 40, 66, 73.

Triumphalism, strength, clarity, certainty have never been prized highly in the Kingdom of God despite all our efforts to make them so. So, at this time, in this place, we are being called to surrender into that strange, humanly unthinkable, dependency on God, watching, trusting. As a Church we must learn once more what it is to be *anawim*, the poor of Yahweh, like that primary model of ecclesial discipleship, Mary, whose place of emptiness becomes a place of life through the power of the Holy Spirit and that power alone.

We must grieve, yes, – for the loss of social status, particularly as priests, which may have served our egos – but we must also dance. We must learn to both grieve and dance at the same time. The future belongs to those who can accept the grief which is truly theirs, and in the midst of the grief, intuit fresh possibility. Christian faith, alive with the resurrection hope, intuits the climate of crisis and grief to be pregnant with the fresh creativity of God. Christian faith is energised with attentiveness to that possibility. The two creation stories of Christian faith – Yahweh's creation of the world and humanity from nothing, related to us in *Genesis*, and the story of the Father's power alive in the new Adam, Jesus, which is related to us in the accounts of the empty tomb – both disclose to us that confusion, darkness, and bewilderment – grief – are the precursors to God doing something new in our midst if we have but the ears to hear and the eyes to see. Indeed, the miracle which awaits us as we keep journeying into this new millennium at a time in which hope and fear, danger and possibility exist in such equal tension, transformed into grief and dance, is nothing other than the re-birth of Christian faith and the revitalization of Christian ministry. Out of our grief and out of our dance will flow new streams of living water.

What enables us to dance? What is the choreography of this dance? What is the music to which our dance responds even in the midst of our grief? It is nothing other than the Eternal Dance of the Triune God. We are being invited to be swept into this dance and to have our ministry choreographed to its rhythm. We are being led into the very life of the

Father, Son and Holy Spirit which is given gratuitously to all people precisely through our ministry. This Table, this Hospitality, is where we are all headed: it is the goal of our life as it is the origin of our life. We are called to have communion at this table. This is why the icon of Rublev has the open space around the table: it is the space for us.

The Table is the Mystery of Vulnerability, Mercy and Possibility. These are not just three characteristics of God. They are the three Persons within the Community of the Godhead, made one because they exist only in virtue of their relationship to each other. In the end, then, God is this extraordinary Mystery of Mutuality. We are called to share in this Mutuality. And we are called to witness to this Mutuality. We care called to live this Communion which we perceive in God's own self so that through us, and the exercise of our ministry, people can begin to glimpse what God is really like – this eternal invitation to Relationship. This understanding of God as Trinity teaches us that we are made for relationship, that we exist in relationship or not at all, that we find our meaning in our interaction with others. We are made in the image of this God, and our ministry is exclusively at the service of this Mystery. The Trinity is not just a wonderful idea; it is a challenge and an imperative to all of us who profess our faith in it, a challenge to minister in a particular way, to relate to each other in an altogether new way.

Karl Rahner once wrote of the word, 'God':

> The concept of 'God' is not a grasp of God by which a person masters the mystery, but it is letting oneself be grasped by the mystery that is present and yet ever distant.[3]

How true this is of the Mystery of God as Trinity. We journey through Christ to the Father in the Spirit into an ever deeper appreciation of the mystery of a Triune God. As we journey into this Mystery, the Mystery itself begins to form us, to shape us, to fashion us, and to direct us.

---

3   Karl Rahner, *Foundations of Christian Faith: An introduction to the idea of Christianity*, translated by William V. Dych (New York: Seabury Press/London: Darton, Longman and Todd, 1978), 54.

We open ourselves to this Mystery, and like Abraham who exercised hospitality to the three visitors in Genesis 18, we find ourselves blessed, changed, opened to unimagined possibility.

The Trinity is our memory waiting to become our future.

The late Irish writer and poet, John O'Donohue wrote, that we 'are not called to propagate an ideology of mimicking a wonderful Jesus. Rather, [we] are called to enter in rhythm with him an imaginative journey to the frontiers where the questions become raw and relentless, to sense the membrane where the awfulness and the intimacy of God meet in each of us.'[4] Keeping our gaze on the Mystery of the Triune God, being ever drawn into its truth and its beauty, may our ministry be for the world the icon of that membrane.

> *I keep asking that the God of our Lord Jesus Christ, the glorious*
> *Father, may give you the Spirit of wisdom and revelation, so that*
> *you may know him better. I pray that the eyes of your heart may be*
> *enlightened in order that you may know the hope to which he has*
> *called you, the riches of his glorious inheritance in his holy people,*
> *and his incomparably great power for us who believe.*
>
> (*Eph* 1:15-19)

---

4   John O'Donohue, 'The Agenda for Theology in Ireland Today I', *The Furrow* 42 (1991), 698.